ruby
slippers

ruby slippers

how the soul of a woman brings her home

jonalyn grace fincher

ZONDERVAN®

ZONDERVAN.com/
AUTHORTRACKER
follow your favorite authors

▪ ZONDERVAN®

Ruby Slippers
Copyright © 2007 by Jonalyn Grace Fincher

Requests for information should be addressed to:

Zondervan, *Grand Rapids, Michigan 49530*

Library of Congress Cataloging-in-Publication Data

Fincher, Jonalyn Grace.
  Ruby slippers : how the soul of a woman brings her home / Jonalyn Grace Fincher.
    p. cm.
  Includes bibliographical references.
  ISBN-10: 0-310-27243-2
  ISBN-13: 978-0-310-27243-4
  1. Christian women — Religious life. 2. Femininity — Religious aspects — Christianity. I. Title.
BV4527.F53 2007
248.8'43 — dc22

                                                                      2007000443

Published in association with the literary agency of Alive Communications, Inc., 7680 Goddard Street #200, Colorado Springs, CO 80920, www. alivecommunications.com.

Some names of individuals have been changed.

Interior design by Michelle Espinoza

Printed in the United States of America

---

07 08 09 10 11 12 • 21 20 19 18 17 16 15 14 13 12 11 10 9 8 7 6 5 4 3 2 1

This book is dedicated to the men who opened doors for me.
My grandfather who opened Grace.
My father who opened Truth.
My husband, Dale,
who propped both doors open
so we might run through them together.

contents

femininity beyond fairy tales

True emancipation begins neither at the polls nor in courts.
It begins in woman's soul.

Emma Goldman

i grew up in a warm but strict family—one that modeled a loving mother and a capable father so convincingly that my biggest and best dream was to marry a man just like my dad and to have a large family. By fifth grade, I knew I wanted to have twelve children, a practical decision based on a formula I had created (Husband + Many Kids = Successful Christian Female) and fueled by too many readings of *Cheaper by the Dozen*.

At slumber parties, my friends and I whispered about our future families. We planned how we would all find our knights in shining armor and have a brood of kids and keep house. And with this brood, we would make an impact such that the world has never seen.

I smugly disavowed college. I supposed it was all right for those who found a career more meaningful than the mothering of young minds, but it was not for me. Friends who intended to go to college didn't fool me either; they didn't really care about the education or degrees or career, they wanted a man. College was just a larger hunting ground. At least I was honest.

But my practical plans gave way to my romantic side, especially when I visited the University of Virginia (UVA) as a junior in high school. Arriving late in the evening, I saw those brick mansions on Rugby Road lit up like enormous jack-o-lanterns, grinning a warm amber welcome. I was enchanted. Years later, when friends asked why I gave up all the excellent, affordable schools in California for UVA, I explained that I was a hopeless romantic and fell in love with the beauty, the serpentine brick walls, the history, and especially those enchanting mansions, which I quickly learned were the raucous homes of fraternity boys. But the practical reason I gave was that I went to study American history where our country's history began.

From Virginia's brick buildings and white-columned architecture, I headed not to the altar but to graduate school at Talbot School of Theology in Southern California, where I studied the philosophy of religion and ethics. All the students at Talbot were required to attend a formal counseling session at the university clinic. The school wanted to determine our psychological health, and since so many graduates of the school would one day be offering pastoral training to church members, the school wanted us to see what it feels like to be on the other side of therapy.

On the day of my session, I sat on a brown-and-yellow-flecked couch, noticeably lower to the ground than the straight-backed chair holding my new psychologist. He had already impressed me with two things: he was uncomfortably close to my age, and he was bald.

I started by sharing some of the things I loved to do and tried to keep the conversation casual and light. He didn't say much, just sat there scribbling notes. After an awkward silence, in which I realized how different this was from other psychology sessions I had encountered, I grew more and more uncomfortable. The man looked down at his yellow legal pad and ventured a single comment: "I notice your interests are feminine." I think it was meant as an enlightening, now-you-can-be-unshackled observation. But I felt accused and bewildered. Femininity had never been a liability before. What now? Should I apologize? He continued, "You sew, knit, paint, play piano, cook, and read. You want a large family." (I still wanted twelve children.) He continued slicing apart some of my favorite activities. As I listened to him, I raised my walls of self-defense.

My eyes darted to the clock — forty-five more minutes of this. It was grueling. Relief flooded me when I finally fled the session, out the glass doors and into my little Toyota painted periwinkle. Periwinkle, is that too feminine?

That afternoon, five years ago, was where this book began. My strange encounter with the psychologist got me thinking about femininity in a way I never had before. What is femininity? Is something wrong with it? Is anything right with it? When I began to think about it, I realized I had been receiving cues about appropriate femininity from my earliest days. My family told me what appropriate women's roles were, my church told me how girls and women should comport themselves, the magazines I read gave me pictures of femininity, even my female teachers at school offered a certain model of femininity. Of course, not all the messages I received about femininity were compatible with one another.

Five years ago, if I had closed my eyes and thought "feminine," I would have imagined makeup counters (where I wasn't permitted to dabble until high school), lingerie (definitely off limits until vows were spoken), corsets, garters, heels, perfume, and wild, wind-blown hair (a stumbling block for men, my mother would say, encouraging me to keep my tresses up and unnoticed). Being feminine meant being subtle, demure, modest, nurturing, matronly, big-breasted, slim-waisted, curvaceously hipped, and, of course, wearing lots and lots of lace. Femininity was all the outer stuff.

By high school, I was good at copying the trappings of femininity. A coworker had once told me, "Never leave the house without lipstick and earrings." I duly added that "rule" to my list. Popular girls didn't wear glasses, so I got contacts after going through seventh grade with bright purple frames. Sexy women always revealed some curves, so I learned to do that as well. Somewhere along the way, fashion and sex appeal, sassy skirts and dangly earrings, knit their way into my understanding of proper femininity.

To confuse matters, I learned from others that femininity was also about being understated, reserved, and gentle, and of course, producing babies. The church and well-meaning women taught me that femininity was associated with behavior. Godly, feminine women did certain things (baked casseroles, attended Bible studies, raised children, and smiled a lot) and didn't do other things (contradict men or have sex outside of marriage). Being feminine was not just a matter of looks, but of behavior and scruples. It was as much about how a woman acted as how she should appear.

For all these people's well-meaning messages, I have found that cosmetics, fashion, and godly behavior do not exhaust womanhood. All those ideas about being feminine are often helpful, and I still affirm many of them. I like to look beautiful. I like dressing in something lacy and modest, yet alluring. I love knowing that my husband will admire my curves. I like attending Bible studies and smiling, and of course, it's incontrovertible that Christ-following women — and men — should reserve sex for marriage.

But this book is an exploration of womanhood that goes beyond such a view of the feminine, to a femininity that is deeper than appearance and action. A femininity that reaches into the fabric of a woman's soul and weaves into our minds, emotions, wills, desires, and spirits. My thinking about femininity is very much informed by what I learned about philosophy and Scripture at Talbot. Under Dr. J. P. Moreland, I learned the difference between a body and a soul. From Dr. Robert L. Saucy, a professor of longstanding dignity, a man of integrity and stubbornness much like Gandalf the Grey, I first learned how the church today may not be treating women like Jesus and the apostle Paul treated them. In his class, sitting two rows back, surrounded by more men than women, I learned that Dr. Saucy thought a woman's role in the church should be at least equal to the vital place women have in the home. This conservative professor actually thought women should speak from the pulpit, not as elders, but definitely as teachers. I walked out of that class on clouds. Could it be possible? Were there more things that women could do without guilt, without being shamed back into their "proper role"?

I also learned to think about femininity and gender roles in my first full-time job.[1] Three months after graduating from Talbot, I began teaching junior high at a local Christian school. Teaching is one of the few occupations where a female can experience equality.[2] In such an environment, I found that I had as much to offer as any of the male teachers, that I could take dominion of my classroom. I was encouraged that if I could teach theology and philosophy to young teenagers, I could teach it to anyone, anywhere. I was regarded with respect among other male employees. I was even consulted as an intellectual and spiritual equal by my boss. That began building confidence into my soul.

But most important, my thinking about femininity has been shaped by my marriage. When asked what she thought of his new girlfriend, Dale's mother matter-of-factly said of me, "She's your equal." That was all the praise he wanted. Dale and I met and married while we were both students at Talbot. After graduation I began my teaching job, which sapped every last ounce of emotional energy I had. At school I could unbelievably exhaust all my verbal needs and come home to a work-at-home husband who wanted to talk. All I wanted was silence. I learned how easily the typical gender roles can be reversed: Dale wanted emotional communion with his new wife, and I was the one who needed time and space to myself, to adjust to all the changes that marriage and teaching had brought.

The next year, Dale and I launched a nonprofit organization together, to minister as a husband-wife team. We longed to bring apologetics into deeper places than thoughts and beliefs, to help people follow Christ with their emotions, wills, spirits, and desires.

We wanted to provide "sturdy answers for better souls," and to help others "become more appropriately human." We called our organization "Soulation," a sort of soul celebration and soul formation all rolled into one. We speak about God's theology for everything, using apologetics, hermeneutics, arts, and history. More recently I've learned how each of these disciplines contributes to the woman's soul.

Soulation is a fledgling experiment that reminds me that Dale and I work as equals. Dale and I are partners in Soulation and partners at home. On plane trips, we hash out new ideas. After Dale speaks, he asks me for feedback: Was he poised? Was his talk well-organized? Was he humble? After I speak, Dale critiques me. Out of one of these talks, he encouraged me to do more than speak about the essence of woman. He said I should write a book about it.

Dale has been my fellow traveler through the woods and fields, the bogs and mountain peaks of understanding femininity, cheering me into these uncharted places, remapping my ideas when he thinks of counterexamples, and refusing to slow his mental energies in our debates. He has shared my confusion when, although we have identical seminary educations, a pulpit is opened to him but barred to me. We have sat together in stunned silence as I am accused of being prideful when I've asked to participate in teaching devotionals. His companionship reminds me of the many ways two can become one, and that I always offer something worth knowing to one man on earth. Through my husband's eyes, I get daily reminders that a man needs a woman, not as a servant or a helper, not as a cook or a nurturer, not as a princess or a nag, but as a woman. My husband, more than that psychologist, more than my family of origin, more than my education at UVA or Talbot, got me thinking more deeply about femininity.

Prescriptions and Lists

Nazi Germany tried to engineer the proper sphere for women in an easy alliteration: *Küche, Kirche, Kinder* (Kitchen, Church, Children).[3] It wasn't too difficult for Adolf Hitler to propagandize these ideas. Most people agreed with him when he said, "There are two separate arenas in the life of a nation: that of men and that of women. A woman's Nature has rightly ordained that men head the family and are burdened with the task of protecting their people, the community. The world of the woman, when she is fortunate, is her family, her husband, her children, her home."[4]

A decade later, the book *Fascinating Womanhood* offered the do's and don'ts of 1950s femininity. A woman should not invade a man's "natural" sphere or try to excel him in anything that requires his masculine ability. Instead she should recognize her husband's superior strength and ability. She ought to focus on being a domestic goddess.

Whether women fulfilled these roles is not the point. They were expected to keep out of a man's domain. Ray Charles belted out a similar idea about his woman: "She knows a woman's place is right there now in her home." Feminine guidance is abundant today; it is regularly updated into modern stuff like what the hot girls wear, what the sexy women do in bed, and what Martha Stewart does for her Halloween parties.

The church has prescriptions for femininity too — only ours are usually more dogmatic and romantic than popular culture's versions. Modern Christian books for women claim that we are naturally more loving and want to be rescued, led, and sheltered. So the books teach us to be more respectful in order to get what our "nature" wants. We are quick to take our cues from others without taking time to know what our nature is.

A dose of small-group Bible studies, a teaspoon of Dr. Laura, and a tablespoon of Oprah, some zest of Beth Moore, and voilà, this is our femininity. We use this concoction of femininity to measure ourselves, our friends, and our foes. Femininity becomes a corset that we stuff our souls into and hope the hooks don't bust open and reveal who we really are. Indeed, modern femininity provides us with several different corsets to choose from. For instance, we can be single, sexy, athletic, maternal, or intellectual. Pop culture—and pop Christian culture—panders to all these stereotypes, and each comes with its own codes of dress and behavior.

The Single Corset

I am punctual, happy, gracious, incredibly excellent at everything I do while I pray fervently for a husband, attend the singles group, and wait and wait and wait. I struggle with sexual desire but put my hope in the promise that God will romance me while I wait for a man. But what if the title "single" vexes me, makes me feel separated and cut off from the church? What if I grow weary of the church's focus on the biological family? Or what if I don't want to be a wife or mother? Should I feel guilty? Is wifehood or motherhood central to my femininity? What if I am divorced and feel afraid that I am less of a Christian? Is there room for me in the body? Can I enjoy being a single female without feeling like I'm a second-class citizen in the kingdom of God?

The Sexy Corset

Get the bronzer and the highlights, the seductive look, what my Aunt Bev calls "bedroom eyes," and the body, toned and shapely. But what if I just want to cuddle after a good cry, when my mascara bleeds, and my T-shirt is baggy and rumpled? Can I still be taken seriously, appreciated, and valued? And then, what if I gain weight and my husband thinks I'm fat? Am I a bad woman? Am I still feminine?

The Mother Corset

I live for my children, drive for my children, shop for and read to my children. Get the minivan, filter out all the "bad" stuff in their lives, be it sugary cereal, Harry Potter, or contact sports. I make a hot supper every evening. But what if I hate cooking? Or what if I want to finish college or go to law school? What if I don't really like being with kids all day long? What if I want to work on something other than long division and laundry? Can I be both a mom and a woman with other interests?

The Christian Wife Corset

I keep a prayer journal and record in it regularly. My fridge is covered in missionary support pictures. I work hard to act submissive (whatever that means) to my man, and let my husband be the spiritual leader. I am a homemaker. I try to act happy, and at night, sexy (if I'm awake and thin enough and interested enough), though I usually feel guilty about how I act and look. But what if I'm bored with church, annoyed with perfect, excellent women, tired of praying for missionaries I don't know, and terribly unsexy and exhausted? What if my husband doesn't care about the church? What if I'm only doing the Bible study to look good? Am I still a Christian woman?

The Working Wife Corset

I work a full-time job and do it better than any guy. I compete for better pay and greater benefits, and eat out all the time. I don't want to learn how to cook, because I don't want another task to complete. My husband and I share a bed, but that's about all. We are waiting to have children until my career is established. But what if I want to have a baby and keep my career? What if I really don't have the energy when I come home to keep up on housecleaning, laundry, meal-making, lovemaking, and entertaining? Am I a bad wife? What if I feel inadequate, even though I only get four hours of sleep every night? Is there something I'm doing wrong? Can I still be a feminine woman?

The Athletic Girl Corset

I work out, run with anyone who can keep up, wear a sports bra as the undergarment of choice, never cry, eat organic, and roar during sporting events. But what if I get teary-eyed or want to show how hurt someone made me? Can I share my feelings? What if I want to wear a skirt and an underwire bra, or eat fast food for a week? Can I without being dismissed as too girly or "letting myself go"?

The Academic Girl Corset

I wear glasses, hang out at coffee shops, carry a book to all events, ask penetrating questions, spar intellectually with the guys, study physics, engineering, or philosophy. But what if I want to shout about my anger, cry over my losses, read a romance novel or a fashion magazine? What if I prefer to attend a baby shower over an academic conference? Can I still be respected by men? Can I still respect myself? Can I claim my womanhood without being dismissed in the academy as over-reacting or a man-hater or too feminine?

We all wear corsets. We often layer them, multiplying their effect, tightening the cords around our soul, until we look culturally appealing, Christianly appropriate, and feel wretchedly uncomfortable. One woman raised in the church put it like this: "I have always been a man-made woman. Am I allowed to do this? Can I say these things? Can I walk this direction?"[5] We are quick to take our cues from others. But regardless of who put us into the corset, we have chosen to keep it; we still wear it. Perhaps we are afraid we will flop around without it; maybe we fear the void it will leave in our lives if it's gone. Who are we without the role of mother or wife? Who are we without our work? What is our value without our accomplishments? We have won the right to be everlastingly unhappy and exhausted, but dang, we look good!

Slippers That Don't Fit

In *Grimm's Fairy Tales*, we find the original version of *Cinderella*, where the familiar glass slipper is actually a golden pair that is, of course, very small. When Cinderella's evil stepsisters fail to fit into these tiny slippers, one stepsister slices off her offensively large heel, and the other, her enormous, protruding big toe. In turn, they shove their mutilated feet into the slippers and stifle their pain and think, "A queen will never have to walk," and limp over to the prince. "Here I am," they say, "good enough to fit the shoe." But the telltale blood filling the golden slipper, spilling out, staining their stockings and marking their footprints, betrays them. A pair of doves sing warning to the prince, "Look at the trail of blood." He turns his horse around and returns the false bride. What the Grimms tell us is that the wicked stepsisters both had beautiful feet, but they cut up something lovely so they might fit the small, dainty, golden slippers — slippers not made for them.

Like Cinderella's stepsisters, I've tried to wear shoes that don't really fit. For proms and formals and evening dinners, I will squeeze my feet into painfully high heels even though I'd rather wear sensible, though "unfeminine" shoes. I endure the evening with cramped, swollen, and pounding feet, new blisters that will heal over the next week, and an annoyance with my foolishness. Still, I keep smiling and announce that these shoes are really so comfortable.

Often the roles we play are like pinching shoes. In order to fit into some role, we squeeze ourselves, contort ourselves, even cut off parts of ourselves. We accept these roles, and the contortions they sometimes demand, and we call it womanly, submissive even. The script for this role might come as a stack of pink pages, in lovely cursive, complete with a lacy edge and pink ribbon. It has already been typed for us, perhaps lovingly by the men in our church or by the father who raised us or the grandmother who blamed us or the mother we still want to please. And we play the part perfectly.

It hurts to wear shoes that are not for us. It hurts to keep shaving off parts of our souls. Can we just admit it once and for all? Our feet don't fit Cinderella's slipper. Most of the time I'm not sexy or a dedicated homemaker or a fit athlete or a successful professional or (and this is hard to admit) perfectly rational. Can I suggest that you aren't either? It's embarrassing — ugly even — when we see what we've done to ourselves to fit something that doesn't even belong to us, but until we admit it, we can't get out of these silly shoes. Finally, we cannot learn that there might be more to us, more to walk into, more to life than our current view of Christian womanhood.

As cultural critic and apologist Elaine Storkey writes, "The frightening thing is that this distorted picture of Christian womanhood, and the unquestioned 'rightness' of traditional roles, has many women in its grip, and prevents them from getting within a mile of growing into maturity and knowing real freedom in Christ."[6]

It's time to remove these stifling shoes and corsets so we can walk closer to Christ.

Ruby Red Slippers

Our femininity shouldn't be like Cinderella's golden slippers — we shouldn't have to contort ourselves to fit someone else's understanding of what it means to be feminine.

Could there be a kind of femininity that is life-giving, not juvenile or overly idealistic, something not constricting, but freeing to our souls? Something Christ might be able to help us find?

Think about one more pair of fairy-tale shoes: the witch's ruby slippers that Dorothy comes to wear in MGM's movie *The Wizard of Oz*. These slippers are like our femininity, something we've been given that we're not always sure we want. When Dorothy puts them on, Glinda says, "There they are and there they'll stay." These shoes weren't what Dorothy was expecting — they are the main source of her continual problems. The Wicked Witch of the West will stop at nothing to claim them because they're powerful. This is where the magic comes in; the ruby slippers cannot be removed unless Dorothy is killed. Dorothy is unaware of her ruby slippers' potential; she has no clue that they're the answer to her deepest problem and her life's quest.

Dorothy's story is like our own. After all Dorothy's efforts are spent, after she's played an unintentional part in murdering the evil witch, after her friends are disillusioned and traumatized by their unsuccessful journey, Dorothy learns she's always had what she needed to get safely home. She learns that she didn't need to work so hard, that her to-do list was way too long. Getting home is surprisingly simple and close.

In our journey for Christian womanhood, how many girlfriends have we seen give up? How many women drop off along the way, disillusioned with the fake Emerald City and the empty powers of the wizard? For all we've seen and experienced, femininity seems a beautiful glitzy present, full of sparkle and attraction, but a sparkle that attracts more trouble than it's worth. We don't know the gift of our ruby slippers; we'd rather keep marching the yellow brick road, find companions to help along the way, and disregard the particular gift we were given upon entry into this world.

We still own a gift nearer than any task we complete or family we build up. We own a gift within, a gift we've carried since conception, and yet a gift that few of us have plumbed to tap its potential. It is our feminine soul. The corsets we wear — the constricting stories about womanhood that many of us have been told since our earliest days — are neither life-giving nor true. What if our true femininity might be able to free rather than imprison us? What if our femininity pointed us back home?

Home is where we belong. We really can be freer than we are; our souls tell us there is something to reclaim, something Christ must redeem in us. Home means acceptance. Henri Nouwen, a Catholic monk and mystic, wrote that home is where he can hear the voice of God saying, "You are my Beloved, on you my favor rests."[7] Home is where we are safe and therefore most alive. Home is where we are free from Wicked Witches of East and West and North and South. Home is where we are released from our own ego condemning us in what we have done. Home is where we relax with the gift we have been given, glad to know and accept and use it. Home is where we return to the God we alienated, the God who still, surprisingly, wants us, the God who made us, the God whose image we bear. Home is when we discover how we fit into his kingdom.

We need to find what lies in these ruby slippers. We don't have to earn it or march along the winding yellow brick road to find it. We have it now. Femininity is something we get to grow, not gain. Author Rob Bell said it well in *Velvet Elvis*: "We achieve and we push and we perform and we shop and we work out and we accomplish great things, longing to repair the image. Longing to find an identity that feels right. Longing to be comfortable in our own skin. But the thing we are searching for is not somewhere else. It is right here."[8]

Femininity is embedded in us, just like masculinity is embedded in men. Our femininity is like a seed in us waiting to be watered; we get to find what we are and watch Christ redeem and grow our femininity into a green sprout, then a slender sapling, and finally a mighty oak. The work, if you could call it that, is to enjoy owning and growing what you already have: the gift of these ruby slippers.

A Woman's Soul: Do You Find It or Invent It?

Femininity is not a veil I wear or pair of heels I put on or a role I play or a corset I stuff myself into. Femininity is not the thing I hate once a month, it is not a collection of fatty deposits, not a style of clothing, or an overabundance of specific hormones. Femininity is a part of my essence, or philosophically speaking, my soul. Femininity is who I am, not merely what I do. Beneath the layers of socialization, indoctrination, education, and posturing, I am female. In our day and age, asserting a soul's femininity—something unalterable by society—is a pretty radical statement. For today, scholars and ordinary women alike debate whether there is any such thing as a woman's "real nature." Ask a women's studies professor at your local university, and she will likely say that no, there is no such thing as a woman's real nature. Rather, we all participate in gender, a "culturally constructed system of meaning."[9] Whether it's the femininity of all things dainty and delicate, or the femininity of being as wild and sexy and lascivious as men, femininity is created, constructed, and socialized into us.

Then there are others who say our femininity is given to us, that our femininity binds us into a group united by our essential womanly nature. If this womanliness is natural, we cannot redesign it at whim, and, in fact, we ignore it at our peril. Because of our sin and brokenness, we might hide it, we might ignore it, we might hate it, but we will always be woman, even if a faded picture of what God originally intended. This is what the essentialists look for, this nature of womanhood.[10]

Being an essentialist means parsing out what is normal or common from what is natural or God-given. God made women to be human in a particular way, and this way may not feel normal to us now. The core characteristics that women own, in virtue of being daughters of Eve, will often be things we have to reclaim and ask Christ to redeem. Our femininity might not be what we want or what we find easy.

When it comes down to it, I believe there are essentially female characteristics, characteristics women share across time and place and culture, characteristics with which God endowed us. But—and here I want to be very clear—I am not arguing for a kind of determinism ("Oh, I can't help that because I'm a woman") or polite, socially sanctioned oppression ("You cannot do that as well because women are gullible and less rational"). This "soul essentialism" is not so much a matter of comparing myself to a list of feminine qualities and limiting myself to them, as it is discovering which feminine characteristics God put in me and allowing Christ to redeem and free me to be a woman. This book is about finding our home, not finding another to-do list. Safety, security, and freedom is what it means to come home.

Consulting the Cobbler

The nature of woman is not, of course, pure and untarnished. It is bent by the judgment of God and by the pockmarks of sin. Yet, Jesus is in the business of redeeming and restoring our true created nature, including our femininity.

To know what femininity is, we must look to our Maker. To know our own souls, we need the Maker of our souls to help us sit honestly with confusing parts of Scripture, things like "women are to keep silent" but "she opens her mouth in wisdom."[11] "I do not allow a woman to teach or exercise authority over a man," and "Deborah, a prophetess, the wife of Lappidoth, was judging Israel at that time."[12] There is the acclaimed biblical view of manhood where the man is to be the provider and protector, and yet we find in the Bible that "she looks well to the ways of her household" or the examples of Esther and Huldah commended for protecting men.[13] One God, the triune Father, Son, and Holy Spirit inspired each of these passages. What does God think about our femininity, about our view of ourselves?

To interact with God on our femininity, we must also know ourselves. We must be willing to discover what is deep inside ourselves, underneath all the roles. We may find femininity is more messy and vibrant, flexible and freeing, and yet less sexy or dramatic than we had expected.

This is why I must come to you first as a woman, not as a philosopher or a theologian, not as a historian or a writer, but as a woman with my bit of experiences, a hamper full of frailties, and plenty of concern. I am a woman who has felt the rejection of the men I love and respect when they told me I did not have the role to speak in the church. Not because of my views, experience, age, or training, but because I am a woman. I have experienced people overlooking my opinion or my ideas in favor of the man's next to me. And because of such experiences, I have felt angry disgust begin to take root in my soul.

Confessing my annoyance and disgust has been the beginning of discovery. The topic of women's differences, like men's differences, is a place like no other, a place where it is much easier to pretend than to confess, though we ache to tell our secrets, to find the scissors to cut open the taut corset strings holding us in, to breathe deep of the air of honesty, without *Good Housekeeping* or our mother's voice sounding judgment in our minds, without the fear of being judged by what we should have done that time, or what we ought to do now. Honesty with the Spirit of Light and the God of Truth, honesty to listen to what God is telling us, honesty to wait to know his original intention for these ruby slippers. This is where we begin.

One important caveat: I am not claiming to have the final words on women. I am not offering an exhaustive index on femininity or the only biblical model for womanhood (though I believe my model is biblically sound). I can't claim to know God's final thoughts on women. But I can claim to know some sure, solid cornerstones: I found that Jesus loves women just as much as men. He has more to suggest and question about current gender ideas than I would have put him up to. He's been defending and dignifying women for millennia. He won't stop. He won't shy away from the gender debate in the church or the attack on his very nature in the resuscitation of gnostic and sacred feminine ideas. He keeps reminding me that there is nothing funny or impossible about female nature.

When we open ourselves up to God, we discover that he has anticipated our open-door policy, that he will not belittle us for our mutilated feet, or shame us for being unable to fit the golden slippers that fit none but the first Eve. He won't become passive-aggressive and blame us with clicking tongue and disappointed eyes, or frown at us as he puts away the pair of shoes we could have worn if we had only made better choices, nor will he scold us for wearing a corset that has never been helpful or true, even though it may have looked good. Instead, we will find him sitting on a lowly bench like a humble shoe-shiner. He will be requesting to remove our painful shoes, to untie the knots and wash our feet. Then we can slip on what he has designed for us.

Because Jesus is a great cobbler, capable of designing scores of different shoes, I will not offer the final words on femininity. There won't be a checklist of feminine traits that are required to make the cut. I can only give a group of family resemblances, flexible soul differences that crop up with women in all cultures and epochs. These family resemblances are only a starter kit, to begin you on a journey of soul care.

Soul Care for Women

At the end of each chapter are soul care questions to pay heed to your soul. These exercises have grown out of questions and thoughts that have both bothered and built me. They are part of the material of my femininity, my identity, my humanity.

During our first weeks of dating, Dale shared with me a new prayer: *The Prayer of Identity.* Its purpose is to help us remember who we are. It is a discipline for our souls, to begin stripping away the layers of our performance ability. These corsets need to be systematically stripped off, because they have tremendous sticking power. The prayer begins with negative statements designed to remove these layers one by one. Take time to write out a prayer for your own soul.

> *I am not a wife, a daughter, a niece, a sister . . .*
> *(your relationships)*
> *I am not a philosopher . . . (your training)*
> *I am not a writer . . . (your job)*

I am not fun, enthusiastic, motivated, organized, disciplined,
  creative … (your gifts)
I am not bossy, demanding, impatient, stubborn, judgmental
  … (your failures)
I am none of these.
I am a naked soul clothed in the righteousness of Christ.

materialism for women

In Hollywood a girl's virtue is much less important than her hairdo.
Hollywood's a place where they'll pay you a thousand dollars
for a kiss and fifty cents for your soul.

Marilyn Monroe

i had been looking forward to this for weeks. Once a month I got to spend the night at my grandmother's house, and this time she had made us matching dresses for our time together. That evening, I dug mine out of my closet. My mother had pressed it, so I would look just right. We were going out to Polly's Pies, where we would eat and talk like ladies. While waiting for our meal, my grandmother would read *Ozma of Oz*, and then at home we would get to read until our heads nodded into our pillows. It didn't matter that I was five years old and fifty years lay between us; my grandmother and I were kindred spirits. She taught me about reading out loud, watching and listening to opera, and all the names of the major streets on the road to her home. We had a special bond, and I adored her.

However, I hadn't planned well enough that afternoon and knew I was going to be late. Grandmother didn't like tardiness. *Dress on, now what?* I asked myself. *Shoes and socks.* I gazed at my dismally small shoe selection. I couldn't wear my tennis shoes with a dress, so that left my blue Mary Jane's. They were the right color, but I had no clean socks. Sensing the clock ticking away, I frantically riffled through my sock drawer and landed on the pair of white lace tights. *These are perfect*, I thought. *They are very proper and elegant.* I wrestled them on, and because I was a few minutes late, I ran to the stairs, slowing down at the top so she could see me walk down gracefully. I wanted to be feminine.

I carefully began descending to greet Grandmother, a commanding woman with silvery, styled hair. She was waiting in her most elegant matching dress. I think she even wore white gloves. *Here I am, ready to love being a lady.* I know I beamed as I walked toward her. My grandmother climbed briskly to meet me halfway up the steps. She wasn't looking at my face; instead she was looking critically at my knees. She bent over to peer more closely.

"Do those need to be washed or are your knees dirty?" She asked in a tone that sounded severe. I looked down, struck with a fresh wash of anxiety.

"I don't know," I said lamely. "I'll go change."

"Nope, there isn't time." Grandmother was already walking back down the stairs. I slowly followed her out the door.

I don't remember having much fun that evening, being too preoccupied with hiding my legs. I was afraid everyone was noticing my ashen knees. Not until I peeled the dirty nylons off did I rest easy again.

It is my earliest recollection of fear about my looks, feeling judged by my appearance. I got an early—I'd say premature—start in worrying over my body, not because I really valued clean knees, but because I craved my grandmother's approval. I wanted to be just like her. She taught me so much: how to sew, how to knit, how to cook, all those things the psychologist had noticed, those "feminine" traits. To this day, I find my grandmother's classy elegance an awesomely high standard. Isn't it in the presence of the great ones that we feel our inadequacies most poignantly?

That night with my grandmother, I learned a powerful lesson about cleanliness in appearance. But I wish that I had learned about my dirty knees and the need for clean tights a little later in the evening. I wish I could have walked proudly into the restaurant with my grandmother unaware of my less-than-pristine appearance. And I wish my grandmother had communicated acceptance, even though I hadn't met her standard of fashion or cleanliness.

The shame of feeling dirty kept me silent for the evening. I remember thinking one thing over and over: I embarrass my grandmother. But I was too afraid of her disapproval to talk about it.

The Creed of Materialism

Have you ever noticed how you feel when a lovely woman walks into the room? One Sunday, I invited my friend Jane to church. Jane is one of the most sensual and lovely women I know. As we stood to sing during worship, she kept looking at our worship leader, who is also quite beautiful. I noticed these two striking women looking at each other several times, checking out each other's clothes and bodies. I'm just guessing, but it wouldn't surprise me if they were comparing, for I was looking at them for the same reasons. The more aware I become of beauty, fashion, and hair, the more aware I become of comparing mine with others.

Back at UVA, a fellow philosophy buddy, Elizabeth, pointed out a girl walking across Jefferson's Lawn. "Look at that," she said. I followed Elizabeth's gaze and saw what she meant: the unflattering tapered pants, baggy around the hips and thighs, tight around the ankles.

"You mean her pants?"

"Yeah," Elizabeth replied, "I used to wear those, until I realized how stupid they look." The damning, self-consciousness had turned my friend into a fashion Nazi. I glanced down at Elizabeth's boot-cut jeans, slim-fitting around her thighs, low-rising around her slim waist. Perfectly fashionable. I unconsciously compared them to mine. And I wished she was still wearing the tapered pants.

When I compare myself to other women, I'm embracing the Creed of Materialism:

Only what I can see is real.
Only what I can touch is real.
Only what I can smell and hear and taste is real.
The visible world is what really matters.

The Creed of Materialism fosters catty competition between women. I'm too busy comparing myself to my prettier or more fashionable companion to be her friend, let alone her sister. Further, the Creed of Materialism asks us to derive our meaning and our sense of worth from the unbidden reactions in other people's faces. Do they think I look good?

Some of us overextend ourselves into fashion, or some of us just give up, certain that our bodies are inadequate, so they're not even worth our time and care. The two extremes, the School of Body Obsession and the School of Body Suppression, are alive and well. One in the overeating, undereating, covering up, fretting and fussing, and the other in some women's determined disregard for valuing their body and appearance. All express our difficulty in owning our bodies.

The School of Body Suppression

When I entered junior high, my hair got "big." It never laid quite right, especially the bangs. The strands that used to be marginally wavy got wiry and immensely voluminous. My hair became too huge and too warm to wear down on hot days because it acted as a sort of burka. Regardless of my attempts with gel and mousse, I ended up with a mane of huge curls (this was before big hair was sexy, before big hair was the basis for a whole cottage industry of Big Sexy Hair products). One sure way of hiding my problem was just rubber-banding the whole head of hair back. So from eighth grade until I graduated from college, I invested in a form of Body Suppression: An army of rubber bands, ribbons, clips, scrunchies, and bandanas. I was so afraid of hearing it called a "fro" that I could not leave my hair down.

The root of my fear came from one morning in eighth grade, when I took a risk and left my hair down. I mustered up the courage to leave the house without a scrunchie. I walked into my homeroom feeling warm and uncomfortable, worked my way through the sea of obviously observing junior high boys and girls, and made it to my desk. Trying to appear collected, I noticed Jeff whisper to his lovely neighbor, Sophie, a girl with sparkly blue eyes and enviable straight hair. With audible disgust, he said, "Look at Jonalyn's hair ... what a fro!"

"Don't be mean," she said with a playful hit.

My twelve-year-old soul withered. He had attacked me where I was trying to be vulnerable. But I didn't look at him. I wouldn't give him the satisfaction of seeing my shame. I tried to appear concerned with the papers in my binder, but my eyes began to fill. I saw nothing. I could only hear his words, again and again, "What a fro!" His words hurt so deeply because he labeled a part of my body and refused to value my soul behind it. He turned my body into a roadblock rather than an informer of my femininity. Worse, he convinced me that my hair prevented me from being feminine; that not just my body, but I, was coarse, unruly, unattractive.

It didn't matter to Jeff that I had spent all morning trying to orchestrate my curls into normalcy. He didn't know I was worried and afraid. He didn't know my soul was aching to be accepted. He didn't know that the effect of his words would keep my hair tied back for more than ten years. He didn't know he was schooling me in materialism, but I learned the creed that day: only what I look like matters.

Ten years later at La Mirada Regional Park, I still believed in the essential ugliness of my hair. I was standing in the shadow of the tennis courts when my date started taking out my hair clip and a mass of bobby pins. It wasn't the first time he had done this. Every date included repetitions of this ceremony and the same question, "Why don't you leave your hair down?" I learned that my hair was more than acceptable to him, that he wanted to see it and enjoy it. He gave me permission to see how my hair, with all its unrestrained curl, contributed to my femininity. I've embraced it.

It took time, but he eventually redeemed my hair. And because of that, among other things, I married him.

The School of Materialism

The fall of my freshman year in high school, my mother gave me a special treat, an all-expense paid trip to JCPenney to get my colors done and experience a long awaited makeover. The middle-aged woman with the strangely tanned skin helped me figure out that I was an autumn. Mercifully, she was right.

That meant that all the bright purples and pinks that looked so good on my mother looked quite wrong on me. It also meant that the oranges and browns that gleamed in older women's eye shadows and glossy, shimmery lips were just right. I groaned inwardly. Shiny, glittery, bronze was not my idea of fun makeup.

The beautician's brown eyes gleamed as she whisked off the fabrics and began applying some mascara. The mascara bristles felt so uncomfortably close to my eyelids that I couldn't keep my lashes from fluttering and causing black to smudge right into the soft skin under my eye. As she fretted over the mistake, I tried to help out: "It's okay, just leave it."

She made a small squeal of protest and admonished me: "You never want to leave a smudge that might make you look tired or sloppy. We always want to make sure we look our best." Wondering why it mattered so much, I sat very still as she daubed with a razor pointed Q-tip. The smudge was gone, a red abrasion in its place. I glanced at my mother who gave me one of her full, but noncommittal smiles. I was having trouble arranging this new experience into my lessons from home. Wasn't it more important to be beautiful on the inside?

Many women struggle with their beauty, even (and I think especially) the beautiful ones. Beautiful women have more to promote, more to preserve, and when they age, more to lose. Some of the most stylish women, whose bodies and fashion I admire and often envy, also sport a skimpy understanding of their value. Perhaps more so for beautiful women, it's easy to confuse beauty for worth. Russian novelist Leo Tolstoy says it's amazing how complete is the delusion "that beauty is goodness." If you aren't beautiful, somehow you're less good, less valuable.

Several weeks after the fro humiliation, Sophie came to school without any makeup. She looked plainer.

"Why aren't you wearing any makeup?" Jeff asked pointedly.

Sophie blushed and looked down. I watched her, remembering that feeling all too well, and I felt my anger rising. Who did this guy think he was? Before she could respond, I retorted, probably too defensively: "Because she knows she's beautiful without it!"

Jeff just ignored me. Sophie, on the other hand, turned those unlined baby-blue eyes away from Jeff and glowed with deep appreciation. "Thank you, Jonalyn."

That day my soul grew out of a small victory. Sophie and I were battling materialism together. It wasn't Jeff so much as his idea that was hurting us — the idea that appearance matters so much, the idea that looks are what constitute your value, that it's not enough to be beautiful on the *inside*, that beauty being found within is the stuff of fairy tales, or as Jim Carrey's character says in *Liar, Liar*, "what ugly people say."

We believe Jim Carrey. In our cities, we still have an aristocracy, not of money, but of beauty. Beauty matters more than soul matters.

In our churches, among people who are to be our family, we vie for it. Beauty is what will get a Christian woman somewhere good and fast; it will bring her romance, it will bring her attention, a husband, and beautiful babies. From adolescence, many Christian girls know the score: girls with good personalities might become missionaries, but they won't get boyfriends or husbands. Pretty girls will get it all, or at least a chance to sign up with rich, successful, loving Prince Charmings. It's the Creed of Materialism disguised as a Christian success story.

Of course, it's not wrong to desire beauty. As C. S. Lewis says, we long "to be united with the beauty we see, to pass into it, to receive it into ourselves, to bathe in it, to become part of it."[1] We want to be beautiful. But sometimes that desire for beauty makes us think beauty is our right or our inheritance as women. And the desire becomes destructive. We begin to envy other women's capacity to captivate. We spend insane amounts of time and money to be equally alluring.

When I walk in a mall, I can see our preoccupation, the proof of female industriousness: how much time and attention we devote to receiving admiration. How much time we spend on perfect curls and skin and accessories. At some point, we must stop and ask why we devote so much energy to this pursuit of beauty. Why do we want to captivate, to hoodwink, to overwhelm with our beauty? Are we trying to vie for more power over the men in our lives? Over other women? Are sunglasses and shoes the best way to prove our value to ourselves?

Getting older doesn't always seem to solve this body preoccupation — our obsession doesn't diminish just because our bodies change and age. In fact, sometimes the wrinkles and sags make us more frantic in our preservation of beauty. Gospel singer Cora Harvey Armstrong, who has plenty of quips on aging, sums it up like this: "Inside every older lady is a younger lady — wondering what the [heck] happened." A woman might have the body of a fifty-year-old, but might still judge herself with the unforgiving standard of a teen. Sometimes I overhear older women greet younger women with comments on their body, their frame, their skinniness. I see envy behind their eyes. Being called "you young thing" isn't necessarily a compliment, especially if it's followed with, "I'm just not as thin as I once was." They are already trying to excuse themselves of some offense. Is this how I will feel as I get older, begrudging the young their lithe frames and taut skin? I would rather be like the grandmother in the novel *Hannah Coulter*, who "remembered her lost suppleness and beauty with affection but without grief."[2] When the time comes, I don't want to grieve the loss of my youth.

The materialist message of our society teaches women that getting wrinkles diminishes their worth, and that their invisible storehouse of soul wisdom, acquired through years of hard living, doesn't really count. Even though Christ died for the rescue and growth of our souls and the remaking of our bodies (not the perpetual youth of our old ones), Christians sneak materialism into the theology of popular books.

Deep down we believe younger really is better! How many Christians are still living the Creed of Materialism, demanding that women be smooth-skinned, creamy-complexioned, full-bosomed, flat-tummied, age-defying goddesses?

Christ can help us understand that as we age, neither our beauty nor our womanhood need be lost. His help and advice is better than that of women's fashion magazines, where articles on aging or physical imperfections are ironically sandwiched between "Secrets for making him wild in bed" and "What's hot for summer!"

Salty Glances

I have dark eyes, in both senses. They are dark brown and they are "darkened." As early as elementary school, I remember spending the Sunday morning church service, the time I was supposed to be listening to the sermon, analyzing and ranking the beauty of each couple at church. I would wonder, *Why is he married to her, he could get a much prettier wife! I would never expect a guy to stay with me if I were that ugly. She's gotten so fat since she married. Her thighs look like cottage cheese. Are her nylons dirty, or is it her knees?*

This glance of comparison isn't always as vitriolic as this. It can begin as admiration. I notice very young girls do it. They invariably stare, not just at women's faces, but at "the outfit." It's open-faced interest, not judgment. I've seen these admiring young eyes turn to their mothers as they try to discretely point out something they like — a scarf, the red shoes, the curly hair. "It's like mine," they proudly say. Beauty is something they enjoy looking at. I remember doing it when I was young, wanting jeans like Christa Purcell or earrings like Mrs. Kentfield. As Anne of Green Gables said, "Imitation is the sincerest form of flattery."

But as I grew older, my eyes darkened, and they have grown accustomed to the shadowy world of criticism.

Many women regularly judge one another's looks: *She shouldn't be wearing that; she's gotten so large since her baby; her lips are too thin; her foundation looks too orange; her legs look like sticks, no tone to them; there's no life in her hair, no vivacity in her eyes.* This is not a modern problem. In *Pride and Prejudice* it comes out of the mouth of Caroline Bingley, who announces that Elizabeth has "no conversation, no stile [sic], no taste, no beauty ... her hair so untidy, so blowsy ... her petticoat, six inches deep in mud!"[3] Caroline takes smug satisfaction in her own pristinely white petticoat.

Modern women do this as well. Materialism teaches us to judge where others are deficient and to try to do better ourselves. The cultural message is drummed into our souls so well that we forget how we've been catechized, our souls trained to obey materialism's Creed.

In Elizabeth von Arnim's novel *Enchanted April*, the exquisitely featured Lady Caroline Dester notices two ordinary women:

> They were really almost quite attractive, if any one could ever be really quite attractive in the wrong clothes. Her eyes swiftly glancing over them, took in every inch of each of them in the half second before she smiled and waved her hand and called out Good-morning. There was nothing, she saw at once, to be hoped for in the way of interest from their clothes. She did not consciously think this.[4]

Today we might notice this unconscious glance at coffee shops, wedding showers, Sunday school, and youth group. Snuggled into a velvet chair, I sip my tea to watch for it at Starbucks. In walks an attractive woman — high heels, red lipstick, full and neatly styled chestnut hair. Nearby women look up and size up the newcomer as she walks by. Oh, we pretend not to notice, feigning sudden interest in the coffee of the day, but the real reason we look up is to check her out. We wait until she passes. Without smiling, we sweep her body in a half-second glance. A sort of sour, dour critical spirit rises up in us, and it's unveiled for a moment in our eyes, an evaluative, salty glance. The more attractive the woman, the higher the heels, the redder the lipstick, the sassier the hair, the more of a threat or interest she becomes. The more I may feel like I could never be that attractive, or that I will buy a belt like hers. I may do a double take. My eyes darken while the woman's back is turned, my eyes force into a smile if the woman turns to me. Like salt polluting clear water, our eyes pollute our souls.

Jesus described the process well, "The eye is the lamp of the body; so then if your eye is clear, your whole body will be full of light. But if your eye is bad, your whole body will be full of darkness."[5] It happens too often, this scrutinizing, salty glance. It's similar to a guy's check-out glance, but women look over each other quicker, and we look for other reasons. The longer the look, the more we confirm what we had initially suspected: "She's better than me," or "She's not as [fill in the blank] as me." We look because we're trying to find out how she measures up against us. Is she competition? Is she prettier? Should I buy that? Would it look better on me? What we're really asking is, "Am I enough?"

Keep track of your gaze when you meet a new woman. Where do your eyes go? Perhaps you appreciate her beauty and are not envious—well and good. But perhaps you compare. How salty are your looks? Can you keep your eyes on her eyes and smile into them, affirming her as a fellow human? Or do you automatically, subconsciously, dart to her body?

Jesus said that if we measure ourselves and our neighbors like this, we will become anxious. "By your standard of measure, it will be measured to you."[6] In other words, when we turn our critical gaze off our friends and onto the mirror, the criticism doesn't cease; instead of criticizing the other women in our church or office, we criticize ourselves.

I cannot check out of any grocery store without paying my dues. The magazines that line the aisles are more than happy to tell me that I'm not measuring up. I get a free education in what the movie stars are wearing, how thin or fat they've become, what mascara they use, and why none of them wear glasses. Standing in these lines, I get to look at them, frozen in one sexy moment after another.

These models are goddesses of today, reminding me that I'm free now, that the ultimate ethic is to be sexually liberated. When I go to the mall and walk past Victoria's Secret, I get to see these free women. Free to wear lacy, ribboned, or patent leather push-up bras with sheer thongs and stiletto heels. Free to look like they're in a perpetual orgasm as they sway their hips out toward me and my husband. Free to do it all in a floor-to-ceiling showroom.

For their freedom, I become enslaved. I may be free to vote and free to learn, free to teach and free to travel, but I am not free to be fashionable and disregard that sexy look. Thanks to marketing, clothing cuts, models, and actresses who double as sex kittens, fashion and sexiness have become inextricably linked.

Trained to criticize other bodies, we gradually turn our critical, dark eyes on ourselves. And that is where many of us are—distracted, discouraged, and embarrassed over our bodies, convinced that we have much to be ashamed of, plenty to suppress. How many women do you know who like trying on swimsuits?

I study my body and have grown vain about my good points and anxious about the bad ones. I've studied and know my friends' bodies. Recently, I saw a website for college students. One button lets you "rank guys and girls" with a cold to hot spectrum.[7] It's a public process, but how many women do this ranking in the privacy of their souls?

In one hazing ritual for sorority membership, the freshman girls are instructed to strip down to their undergarments and lie on the floor. After each girl is blindfolded, the older sorority sisters welcome in a herd of fraternity upperclassmen. The raucous, intoxicated males are outfitted with black permanent markers and told to label the cellulite areas of each girl's body. They charge into the room, turn the lights on, and begin flipping the blindfolded, nearly naked bodies in their orgy of ranking, circling, and labeling.

Afterward, the girls are freed, given their clothes and released to go home and inspect their labels. Though the ink will eventually rub off, the damage is permanent. It's not just the men's fault either. The senior sorority girls will sometimes conduct other status-deciding activities like "boob ranking" where every "sister" is lined up topless according to breast size.

This crass, outrageous objectification is more extreme than what we do to one another every day, but the difference is one of degree, not kind. Many women walk to the beat of men like Dave Matthews, offering what he wants: "Baby ... hike up your skirt a little more / and show your world to me."[8] Don't we do that? We hike up our skirts to fill his eyes with our bodies. Trade in our bodies and we get noticed. Wear this and we might get that guy to stare. Buy that purse and these sunglasses, and men will look longer as we sit across from them at the stoplight. We might even buy something, a car, a dress, a pair of earrings, because it "turns heads." It won't cost much, just our bodies. It's just an act, a role, it's not really us. We believe we can keep our souls intact. But our souls form themselves to this body mold. Our clothes and style teach others how to treat us and tell a story about how we treat ourselves.[9] If we only feed ourselves materialism, our souls are left with nothing to grow into. Our souls cannot grow beyond this limited corset.

The School of Soul Care

It's not that I don't care about clothes and style. Body care is an essential part of being human. Part of the redemption we find in Jesus is the redemption of our broken bodies.

Most of us, however, don't neglect our bodies; what we suffer from is neglect of our souls. We leave our insides shrunken, flabby, and filthy. We're like the headstones at a grave, cleanly chiseled with order and strength, but beneath and within, we are full of dead bones, rotting from the inside out.[10] Faithfully we disregard discipleship; we build our bodies and neglect our souls. We are like the wasp that George Orwell described:

> I thought of a rather cruel trick I once played on a wasp. He was sucking jam on my plate, and I cut him in half. He paid no attention, merely went on with his meal, while a tiny stream of jam trickled out of his severed esophagus. Only when he tried to fly away did he grasp the dreadful thing that

had happened to him. It is the same with modern [wo]man. The thing that has been cut away is [her] soul.[11]

I know my soul has been hurting. It whimpers that something isn't right, and it tries to warn me that our culture's obsession with appearance is cutting into me, that I need more than I'm currently feeding myself. Jesus said we must first clean the inside so that our outsides may become clean as well.[12] Jesus might say our contemporary culture gets it backward: cleaning the outside with another book, another coffee, a new job, a new home, a new guy, a new meal, a fresh outfit, a new pet, a new devotional book, even another Bible study, but we neglect our souls.

In our obsession with beauty, we neglect our very selves. A litany of questions presses in on us. Why do you suppose gray hair and wrinkles make us afraid? Why do we hate buying bathing suits? Why do we feel discouraged after reading a romance novel? Why do we prefer male to female company? Is it just self-loathing or are women really worse companions? Why are we embarrassed of our femininity? Why do we feel unsatisfied? Why can't we control our emotions? Why can't we be good, loyal, creative, faithful friends? Why can't we be content with our friends, our husbands, our sex lives, our intimacy, our house, our children, our income? What is wrong with us?

Perhaps we need to live as if Christ cared for more than our bodies. What if we lived as if Christ wanted to redeem our souls? What if we paid attention to the insides even half as much as we accessorize our outsides? What if we turned our attention away from the mirrors, away from others' comments, away from over-regard or disregard of our bodies, and began attending to our souls?

We could enroll in the School of Soul Care, a school that specializes in everlasting, unseen, real souls. The School of Soul Care has a gracious acceptance policy, one that accepts dirty knees, broken and corseted bodies, smudged mascara, overweight and underweight women. There is no favoritism at this school, for, as the Headmaster says, we all need help and we all are worthy enough to enroll.

Early Catechism

When I was six years old, I loved wearing my white patent leather shoes. One Sunday morning, glad to be wearing clean, white tights, I bounded down the stairs into the kitchen, "Hi, Daddy! How do I look?"

In his quiet and steady manner, he stopped pouring his cereal and looked down at my ballerina pose. "You look very beautiful, Joni." He looked in my eyes, "But do you know what's more important than being beautiful on the outside?"

"What, Daddy?" I chirped as I climbed into my chair.

He paused and then, seriously and intentionally, said, "Being beautiful on the inside."

It was a lesson he repeated until I was in high school, and it was a cornerstone in my growth, something I would depend on to strengthen me in the moments when I doubted my body's beauty. In a sense, my father's words counterbalanced the judgment my grandmother had offered just a few months before.

Recently, I asked my dad the philosophy behind what he used to say. He told me that he had noticed the way women spend their entire lives competing over their looks. "I knew you could never win. Not because you're not beautiful, Joni," he added, "but because no one wins that game."

Soul Care

1. Who taught you that your body matters so much?
2. Who teaches you today about body care? What lessons about body image have you learned from pop culture?

3. Take inventory today on how many times you look in the reflective glass (mirrors, windows, storefronts). Could you go a day without looking in the mirror? Why not?

4. Do you find yourself regularly assessing other women's looks? Comparing yourself to them? Do you then turn your critical gaze on yourself?

5. How do you respond to the idea that God accepts "dirty knees, broken and corseted bodies, smudged mascara, overweight and underweight women"?

6. Jonalyn received a powerful, positive early catechism about her true worth from her father. Reflect on the early catechisms about beauty and self-worth you received.

uncorking the soul

A mole / Digging in a hole / Digging up my soul now /
Going down, excavation.

Bono, U2

my parents gave me a promise ring when I was thirteen. I wore
that ring as a sign of commitment to keep my sexuality sacred
from backseat romps and casual hookups. It was a sign that I had
already pledged my sexual purity to my God and to the possible future
husband I dreamed about.

God gave us all a sign, something between us and him, that all
of our being belongs to him—not just our sexuality or our Sunday
mornings. Our souls are a promise ring, marking the value God gives
to us.

God came to earth not because he wanted to show up like a
cosmic superman, but because he wanted to redeem the souls he gave
us. He found us worthy of his redemption. If we have such a treasure,
isn't it time to know what a soul is? What is it he found worth his
time, his incarnation, his death, his resurrection, and his seal of the
Spirit?

I imagine God upon a loom, the first time he interwove matter
with soul. "See," he said, showing his work to the angels, "I am making something new, matter and soul together reflecting me." And
we became living souls, a body-soul fabric—the woven burlap of

humanity. We are in some ways common because there are billions of us, but we are exquisite too. Humans are like antique silk lace; we are tightly woven, intentionally knotted, and looped and tied strands of body and soul. God's pattern for human beings was distinct from the makings of any other creature. We are material and immaterial, body and soul.

Because we are souls who have bodies, our souls cry in anguish when someone we love dies. We were meant to enjoy the fabric of body and soul tightly woven together, without any cutting out of soul from body. Isn't death a sort of cutting, an unraveling of the fabric God once wove and knotted together?

Our immaterial souls are made to be united with a material body, which is the original pattern that God designed for man and woman. It's a much bigger, fuller gift than we may now know. Our souls are not flimsy, ghostly things. Our souls are not merely handy when we die. They are who we are now. Once we recognize the real meaning of our souls, we can begin to think constructively about all the potential and power in *women's* souls.

Soul Wine

The "soul" is like red wine, grown mature but neglected in a cool, abandoned cellar. To open up the soul is as potent and rich as opening up a bottle of rare wine. If our souls have been shaped by the hands of a living God, what kind of capacities did he put in us?

Jesus told stories to help people understand God's engagement with humans. In the parable of the sower, he explains how people's hearts, or their immaterial souls, are like the soil—hard, rocky, thorny, or rich. "But the seed in the good soil, these are the ones who have heard the word in an honest and good heart, and hold it fast, and bear fruit with perseverance."[1] Jesus treats our souls as if we have the power to be receptive or hardened, to shun or receive God, and depending on who we are, we will shrivel or take root. The soul is the site of decision making; it is where love begins. "You shall love the Lord your God with ... all your soul."[2] Jesus is talking as if our souls are more useful, more pivotal than an extra parachute for our heavenly adventure. He's speaking like our souls are essential to the life he is offering.

Deep down, we at least know our souls are more important than ghostlike things; we reveal it with our language. "I did some soul searching" or "She moved my soul." But because the soul has been dismissed in the academy, in the sciences, in business, it is easy to believe that our souls are nothing more than a marketing gimmick, used in advertising, but less substantial for real life.

Hairy Image Bearers

God made us, it is true, but he also made cucumbers and sycamore trees. The redemption of human souls was worth Christ's thirty-something years on earth not only because God made us, but because God put something divine in us. We're not gods, but we are Godlike.

Understanding our soul helps us understand who God is. God is not physical, but neither is he a thin ghost or shadow, nor is he unconnected to reality. I recall one psychology professor challenging his entire lecture hall of four hundred undergraduate students to explain what it meant to be made in God's image. When no courageous souls stood up, he paused dramatically.

"If you were made in God's image, then God has a body. Do you really believe God has armpit hair and goes to the bathroom?" With one smooth joke, he managed to undo years of Sunday school work. "Therefore," the professor announced with his intelligent, Ivy-League trained mind, "you can't take the Bible literally."

And no one challenged him. He was the first diehard materialist to ever confront my ideas of Christianity. He also had no idea about God's immaterial soul.

Jesus said God is spirit, and we must worship him in spirit. Put another way, God is a soul, and we must worship him as souls, not just as bodies. When Jesus said God is spirit, he was using the old meaning of spirit—an immaterial being.[3] God does not have any physical parts.[4] To be made in God's image may mean a great many things, but one thing is certain—it doesn't have anything to do with our body parts. God does not have a body; there is something about us, something beyond our bodies that resembles God.

A penny bears Abraham Lincoln's image because there are some resemblances between the two, but the penny isn't identical to Lincoln. We bear God's image because we bear some resemblance to him, not in our bodies, but in our souls. Our soul sign links us back to our Maker. "Then the LORD God formed man of dust from the ground, and breathed into his nostrils the breath of life; and man became a living being [soul]."[5]

The Godhead wove our bodies into our souls. We love communing with, creating for, and loving God because God also loves, creates, and communes. God expects it. "Prosper! Reproduce!… Be responsible for the fish in the sea, the birds in the air, and every animal that moves on the face of Earth."[6]

When Jesus tells us to "love the Lord your God with all your heart and with all your soul and with all your might," he assumes we still have that working, creating, communing, loving soul intact. We can love because we are made in his image.

Divine Humans

God is Spirit, but he is not lifeless or dull. God's life ripples out through all of his interesting thoughts, creative choices, full desires, and textured emotions. In God, all things hold together, enduring because of and for him.[7] This sort of energy and vitality and personhood is in smaller measure given to every human. The Hebrews called this life force the soul (*nephesh*) or spirit (*ruach*) of God.[8] *Nephesh* is also translated to mean psychological states in humans, like emotions (Deuteronomy 21:14), choice (Proverbs 21:10), or desire for God (Isaiah 26:9).[9]

Since Scripture often uses "soul" to mean an immaterial life or self, a self that can think, choose, and feel, I will use soul in the same way. The soul is you, the "you" that thinks, feels, and chooses. Christ meant this immaterial "you" when he said, "And you shall love the Lord your God with ... all your soul."[10] Essentially he's saying, "Love me with all the life you've got."[11]

The template or model for our life is God. Everything good about our souls is something God originated. As the trailblazing Christian philosopher Alvin Plantinga put it, "God is the premier person, the first and chief exemplar of personhood ... and the properties most important for an understanding of our personhood are properties we share with him."[12] We are smaller pictures of God. We live because he lives. We think because he thinks. We believe because he believes. We feel because he feels. We love because he first loved.[13]

God feels things: "The LORD was sorry that He had made man on the earth, and He was grieved in His heart."[14] God has thoughts: "My thoughts are not your thoughts."[15] "How precious also are Your thoughts to me, O God! How vast is the sum of them!"[16] God has beliefs: "There is no one like [Job] on earth, a blameless and upright man."[17] God has desires: "When it is My desire I will chastise them."[18] God makes choices: "I ... have chosen this place for Myself as a house of sacrifice."[19] "Behold, My Servant, whom I uphold; My chosen one in whom My soul delights."[20]

God knows every good aspect of our souls and then some.[21] We are just small souls compared to God and can only handle a small portion of his soul characteristics. God is "bigger," so he can handle more good, more love, more intimacy, more choices, more emotions. God enjoys the satisfaction of all his thoughts being true, all his beliefs spot-on, all his desires oriented toward good, and all of his "willings" accomplished.[22] His life is a picture of what we long for, and hence what we long to worship.

God never had a beginning, naively wondering, grasping for knowledge and wisdom. Other than Christ's emptying stint of thirty years, God's soul regularly experiences limitless life: knowledge, pleasure, interest, freshness, intimacy.[23] The incarnation is such an emptying, humbling act because of how much interesting, good stuff Christ emptied out of himself, all in order to redeem our souls to choose more good.[24] With Jesus, we have more freedom to choose the good, the true, and the beautiful. We can taste the power of the divine in our everyday choices. When I plan a new tier in my garden, I'm exercising a Godlike ability, freedom of will. I can choose. My Welsh Corgis don't have that ability, not to will their own good, plant a garden, or stop rolling in dead snails.

What Can Our Souls Do?

I don't just have a soul, like I have curly hair; I am my soul. My soul is me, and I own all my soul's abilities and experiences — memories, emotions, thoughts, beliefs, introspections, desires, choices, sensations. To make it simpler, all my soul's abilities can fit into five categories or capacities: mind, where thoughts and beliefs work; desires, where our attractions and dislikes are pushed and pulled; feelings, where sensations and emotions play; the spirit, where we introspect and meditate; and the will, where our choices begin.[25] Our soul is the keeper of these five capacities.

These five capacities are always with us, whether we're able to use them or not. Every human (man, woman, child, fetus, a patient with Alzheimer's or in a coma) has these capacities. We might not use our ability to think or choose, for instance, when we're sleeping or unconscious, but the capacity is still latent in our souls.[26] These capacities are what make us God's image bearers. And the beauty of being an image bearer is that no one can ever remove our capacities from our soul.

What Lives in Your Soul?

Let's explore the soul's five capacities in a little more detail. The mind thinks and knows, like a judge sitting in her high box, listening to evidence, weighing the rationale, observing the changes. Feelings sit at the bottom, where they ought to be, in the servant role. Desire sits near feelings, will, and mind, because sometimes desire is felt (feelings), sometimes it is chosen (will). Our will controls the whole set of capacities, directing, ordering, controlling, so it sits in the center. Spirit is our ability to think about our soul's capacities, to evaluate our mind, will, feelings, and desire. I've drawn up this model from pooling and reordering the thoughts of J. P. Moreland, Dallas Willard, and Richard Swinburne.[27]

Mind

Mind is my mental capacity; it's what I use for the most mundane to the most complex thinking, believing, and imagining. When I think about how disappointing the King Tut exhibit was, I'm using my mind. When I believe in Jesus's resurrection, I'm using my mind. When I imagine the way my dream home will look, I'm using my mind.

Thoughts are the soul's transportation. Thoughts can take us forward or back in time, they can remove us from the mundane in daydreams or night dreams, they can take us into imaginary worlds in fiction. Thoughts help us imagine life with less or more; they propel us to places and times that trigger our empathy or compassion.

But our thoughts are easily scared away. They enter our souls uninvited and leave unannounced. It is their nature to be fleeting, which is why we lose our train of thought. Thoughts are the running marquee in our soul.

When a thought gets more evidence, it grows up and becomes a belief. With study and experience, certain thoughts grow into beliefs. All our beliefs provide our worldview. I might think, "I hate my thighs." The thought will not stick around unless I have evidence to grow it into a belief. I may go to the beach and watch someone point and laugh at my legs, and then I will stare at glossy, smooth-thighed women in a magazine for a half hour. The thought might lurk around even longer as I look over my sunburned body. I might feel that I hate my thighs. There's not much more growing to do before the seemingly short-lived thought becomes the belief, "My thighs are fat and ugly." The belief is now part of my worldview, so it colors everything I see. I will continue to judge other women according to this standard, and I will buy clothes that disguise my perceived inadequacy. This is what beliefs do: they tell me what is important, what I should do, where to go, what to change. Beliefs, whether true or false, guide me through reality.[28] If I have many true beliefs (meaning my beliefs line up with the way the world is), then I am wise. If I have many false beliefs, I am foolish.

Because beliefs form the permanent backdrop of our souls, they're worth attending to, understanding, and analyzing. Our beliefs can be wrong, even though we hold them with evidence, conviction, and persistence. Every woman must attend to her beliefs and seek out the inconsistencies and inadequacies in order to grow into truth. Beliefs, unlike thoughts and feelings, are stable and long-lasting guests in our souls.

Feelings

Though we use "feeling" to mean both sensation and emotion, these are in fact different types of feelings. When we say, "It won't hurt my feelings," "feelings" means our emotions. If we put on a fur coat and say, "I feel warm," "feelings" means our sensations. Often sensation and emotion arrive together. I get a paper cut, I feel pain (sensation) and annoyance (emotion). The difference is in the origin of the feeling. Emotions—like fear, anxiety, anger, joy, frustration, delight, impatience, and peace—originate in our soul. Sensations, or feelings of the body, usually come to us through our five senses: sight, smell, taste, touch, and sound.[29] Sensations bring the material world into our soul; they're like the newsflash of our bodies, sending direct awareness to us about the juiciness of a tomato, the soft fuzziness of a baby's head, the dripping of rain, the smell of sweet peas. Our soul organizes all the chemical signals and neural firings into a united experience so we can enjoy one united experience: "This tomato is juicy," "This baby's head is soft," "The air feels damp."

Feelings provide the color for our lives; they wash us in emotions and sensations. When we read a love story, when we watch a movie, when we kiss a man, and when we take a bubble bath, we experience feelings. Feelings motivate us to get up and volunteer, buy the CD, return our neighbor's wallet. In the story of the good Samaritan, it is the feeling of deep pity that moves him to behave in kindness; the Gospels record Jesus feeling compassion before performing healing miracles. America's first systematic theologian, Jonathan Edwards, wrote, "If our emotions are not touched, we will not change." If we hear a lecture or a sermon and our feelings are not engaged, we will leave the church or lecture hall and forget we were there, but if our feelings are engaged, we will respond, and our wills begin moving, changing. We work with the Spirit of God and see transformation. Some of us are very aware of our feelings, and some of us don't feel as quickly or as deeply, but we all have feelings. Feelings aren't optional.

Several years ago my family organized a group outing to Pasadena to hear the Philharmonic Orchestra play a tribute to John Williams. A young violinist was going to play three pieces from *Schindler's List*. She took center stage and immediately arrested my attention. She was young but moved with age and solemnity, as if she carried the weight of the Jewish pain in her beautiful body. I could see it from my seat in the seventy-fifth row.

Her violin sang out a dissonant Jewish rift clashing against the inexorable march of the symphony—forward, forward, ever forward. Her hands pushed the bow to make clear, clean tones within the painful melody. The music had the power to transform me; the sound moved me. This American violinist transformed, she became a Jewish woman, her fingers like slender, pliable roots, digging deep down into the violin. We got to watch her pull life out of her pain.

Then the music changed. I looked down at my program: Jewish Town (Krakow Ghetto—Winter '41). I looked back at the gleaming stage; the young woman holding us all in the emotional trance of her music became a young Jewish woman, driven without explanation into the gas chambers. The beauty of her creamy skin, her bare neck, revealed her youth, her frailty. She was wearing golden sandals, and the color so closely matched her skin that she seemed barefoot, one of the young women walking to slaughter, like a lamb taken for a sacrifice. The violin squealed its final high pitch and was silent.

I had been touched. I had been changed. But then it was over. The music, the emotion, and the sensation only live in my memory. Feelings are like that—fair-weather friends. We eagerly invite them into our souls, and they drench us in the intensity of the moment, and then they leave. Then we're left hungering for the experience again. Sometimes that hunger motivates me to replay the scene, re-read the passage, eat another brownie, or close my eyes and press repeat on the CD. Like a wood fire, feelings always need replenishment. They are the other running marquee in our soul. They need the stability of their soul sister: desire.

Desire

Certain things draw us, catching us in their tractor beam, inclining us toward or away from something. These are desires, anchoring points, giving purpose and direction in our soul.

I have long desired to be a kind wife. I sometimes feel like it, and it's no problem to listen attentively to Dale's ideas, or to be patient when I notice something undone that I wished done. My emotions are working *with* my desire. I love those moments. At other times, I don't feel like being kind. If I have chosen to build up my desire to be a kind wife, then my desire will be strong enough to carry me through the impatient or dissatisfied emotional storm. And I won't act out on my unkind emotion. But sometimes my desires are too weak and I'm a passive follower of my emotions—I'm just plain mean, demanding, manipulative, and unhappy. And my husband, Dale, will often jump through hoops trying to please his unappeasable wife.

Desires are companions, sticking with us even after our feelings are gone. This is why good, wholesome desires are worth building up; they hang around longer and stabilize us during emotional storms. Wholesome desires are the lifeboats in our soul, keeping us afloat amidst the turbulent emotional storms. They give us a place to prepare, tie down, and hold out during the unpleasant gusts and hurricanes of feelings. They stabilize us in the wild and triumphant rapids, reminding us that—no matter how wretched or glorious—this too shall pass.

Will

Our will is the central driver or CEO in the soul. The will is often obeyed, but—as any CEO knows—never perfectly.[30] With our wills we can choose and cause things to happen. When the will directs all my capacities, my immaterial life is pleasant—my emotions are governed, my beliefs are based on truth, my thoughts are ordered, my sensations are wholly pure, and I develop the virtue of self-control. Those are great days.

But often, too often, my will is usurped by clamoring appetites, passions, and thoughts. When my emotions dominate me and my desires are too weak, my will is also weakened. It's like skipping a few days of training for a race. When I refuse to exercise my will, I actually weaken my "will muscles." And trying to pick up my training the next day will be all that more difficult.

It's easy for us to say that our emotions are too strong, that I'm just too bitter or in love or annoyed to do any differently. But if we ride the wave of emotions, we have no understanding of their force, nor do we know our own potency to understand and stand up to them. The best way to know our strength of will is to stand up to our own emotions, as Paul said, to buffet our bodies, to run the race well, to reach for the way out of this temptation.[31] Not as a way to earn God's favor, but to make use of the strength he's given us. After all, grace is not opposed to effort; it's opposed to earning.[32] We can learn how to fight our anger and bitterness, lust or disdain, and to eventually grow out of even feeling such hurtful emotions because we push against them, building our will muscles, growing healthy emotions.

Our wills are not just so we can be good little girls, meek and mild. With our wills we enjoy freedom and creativity, to show the world what it means to be women who are free to do what is good, to choose among the many God-honoring ways to act.[33] With our wills we can let the world know what God looks like, what he would do in a situation, how he would look in female form. And herein lies our battle—to will and to work for God's good pleasure.[34]

In high school, Zachary was one of my fun, spontaneous friends who happened to be male. That never made a difference to me, and I grinned over my good luck at his friendship. He guaranteed a nonstop whirlwind of excitement, with stunning Italian good looks and quick wit. Zachary wasn't intimidated by my questions, and he made me laugh. He was also safe—I could hang out with him without starting the gossip chain. He wasn't attracted to me. We spent most of our time talking about his crushes on other girls. And even though Zachary was a heartthrob of most of my girlfriends, I got to enjoy the fun of hanging out without feeling reduced to his obsessive, sporadic romances. We bicycled together, went to church together, debated theology together, and provided running commentary on each other's dating life.

One night after a football game, I sat with Zachary long after the game's scoreboard had buzzed out. I closed my eyes and dozed against the back of the cement step. A light movement on my face jolted me. As I opened my eyes, I could only see Zachary very close, gently stroking my face. My stomach flipped over in bewildered pleasure. He smiled unflinchingly at me. I felt both betrayed and happy, teetering on the precipice, knowing exactly what he wanted, but feeling rather unprepared.

Then I remembered Charlotte Bronte's *Jane Eyre*, and how Jane's passionate strength of will and desire for purity carried her through her own passion toward Mr. Rochester. I chose to walk toward Jane rather than toward Zachary.

I looked Zachary dead-on and drew his hand away from me, laying it back on his side of the bench. In a split second he had changed everything. I knew he didn't really like me, that he was playing with me, but still, it was so hard. Trying to keep the quiver out of my voice, I managed to whisper, "You need to be careful."

"I know," he smiled and then moved his face close to mine—too close—and whispered, "But don't you just, sometimes, wanna have fun?"

Every feeling in my body shouted at me to give in. I wanted him to think I was fun. I wanted a good, long make-out session right then and there, and I wanted to lose myself in his touch. It seemed so good. But I could hear Jane Eyre's words, "Laws and principles are not for the times when there is no temptation; they are for such moments as this ... Preconceived determinations are all I have to stand by, there I plant my foot."[35]

I mustered all sixteen years of my will's strength, stood up, and walked out of that stadium. Sometimes the best thing feels like the most unnatural thing in the world.

Spirit

Our spirit is the capacity we have to know ourselves, including all our capacities.[36] In Scripture, "spirit" can be a synonym for soul, evil spirit, Spirit of God, heart, emotions, or will.[37] And spirit sometimes means our ability to introspect, to look at our other capacities; it is the God-given spotlight or conscience in our souls. Solomon wrote, "The human spirit is the lamp of the LORD that sheds light on one's inmost being."[38] Our spirit is the lamp God uses to show us more about ourselves. "But it was to us that God revealed these things by his Spirit. For his Spirit searches out everything and shows us God's deep secrets. No one can know a person's thoughts except that person's own spirit."[39]

After finishing seminary, I went to professional counseling again. This time, however, I chose a female counselor who had incredibly good references. After several meetings, she suggested I pick up a book by Harriet Lerner called *The Dance of Anger: A Woman's Guide to Healing Her Most Intimate Relationships*. It focuses on the ways women use their strengths to hurt others, and it spoke to my soul, particularly my spirit. There was one part that seemed to leap off the page. "Diagnosing the other person is a favorite pastime for most of us when stress is high. Although it can reflect a wish to provide a truly helpful insight, more often it is a subtle form of blaming and one-upmanship."[40]

Her words shone light into me as if my spirit had turned on a 100-watt bulb that was now beaming into my soul. The Spirit of God revealed my hidden motives, things I was unconscious of, until then. I had diagnosed others' problems and set myself up as their judge. Seeing the truth helped me change.

How Much Is a Soul Worth?

You are a soul; you have a body. And all souls own these capacities. It is in this that we bear the image of God and in this we are all equal, all of us—female, male, single, widowed, married, divorced, young, old, disabled, sick, healthy, or strong. Because we are all created in God's image, we all own souls, we are all little mirrors of God. In our souls we are equally endowed from our Creator with certain capacities.

Edith Stein was a Jewish woman who converted to Catholicism, became a Carmelite nun, and was eventually killed at Auschwitz. She pointed out, "Humanity is primary, femininity is secondary." In our humanity, men and women are equal.[41] We are united in that we are all souls. As Stein experienced, our souls do not guarantee that we will be treated as image bearers or that we will know the depth of our soul's capacities or even that we will allow Christ to redeem all our capacities. But it means we have souls made in God's image, nonetheless.

Bearing the image of God is both a gift and a task. Like Dorothy who was gifted ruby slippers but still had to use them to realize their potency, we have been given capacities in our soul. It is our task to grow the image that was placed in us. We participate by receiving God's grace, watching him as he mends our souls, joining him by submitting all our capacities for his renovations.

When I first heard Josh Groban's music, I knew I had found a kindred spirit. He takes the time to renew the meaning of old songs. He treats them as gems of antiquity, with reverential, full-bellowed sound, and measured pace. It was while listening to his rendition of "O Holy Night" that I realized afresh the depth in these well-worn words:

Long lay the world
In sin and error pining
'Til He appeared
And the soul felt its worth.[42]

God revealed his value for our souls when he reached toward us in Christ—the Son of God bearing the image of God. Christ is the Teacher, schooling us to know the worth of our souls, the way both men and women were made to bear the image of God.

Soul Care

1. What does it mean to be made in the image of God?
2. Draw a picture of a coat rack with five hooks. Label each hook with one of the five capacities. List examples for each capacity from your life.
3. Attend to your mind. What are some beliefs you hold right now about your femininity? About your body? About your value in the church?
4. Attend to your feelings. What do you feel when you hear: "role," "homemaker," "helper," and "femininity"?

5. Attend to your spirit. Read Psalm 23 and ask God to help you with the truth, "He restores my soul." What capacity of your soul most needs restoration?

6. Read Mark 7:21; 2 Chronicles 15:15; Jeremiah 29:13; and Psalm 16:7–9. Determine which soul (sometimes called "heart") capacity is being mentioned.[43]

the same planet

*Although almost everyone would agree that men and women are
different, how different is still undefined for most people.*

John Gray

Since 1993, John Gray's book *Men Are from Mars, Women Are from
Venus* has sold millions of copies. Gray's ideas are firmly lodged in
our cultural landscape: his planetary dichotomy pops up in marriage
conferences, fashion magazines, most Christian gender discussions,
and book reviews about gender relations. His hypothetical, mytho-
logical thesis has wiggled into our foundational beliefs about gender:
Men and women are different enough to make us nearly different
species. It's like we're from different planets altogether.

Venus dwellers all have degrees in psychology and spend their
days listening and relating to each other, changing their outfits
depending on their mood because they value love, communication,
beauty, and relationships. They get their sense of self from their feelings and the quality of their relationships. Martians, on the other
hand, get their sense of self from their ability to achieve results, which
is why they wear uniforms to reflect their competency and power.
Martians value efficiency, power, and achievement, and they never
study psychology.

The problem? There are men who value psychology and women
who love power. No men I know—not my husband, my dad, my

brother, or any of my male friends—fit Gray's Mars model, nor do many women of my acquaintance act like true Venusians. Gray's stereotypes suggest that females only care about relationships, and males only value achievement, when in reality, plenty of men and women care about both.

Men and Women Are from Planet Earth

We have forgotten a different, better story of our beginning. Once upon a time, God created Man and Woman to live on the same planet. In this story, when Man feels deficient in companionship, Woman arrives on the scene. They spend time together willingly; there were no women's conferences or men's BBQs. They got along fabulously, and when the day was over, they decided to spend the night together. Then they woke up together and decided to continue working alongside each other. In fact, their Creator told them they should work together. The next night they slept together again and lived in the same garden, sharing the jobs. Then one day, they ate the fruit, together.

All this togetherness, all this partnership, may seem shocking to a culture steeped in Martian men and Venusian women—but it's the original story and one Christians claim as truer than Gray's myth. We've come to believe men and women are drastically different, but as our story says, we were created to be together. In fact, Man was told by the most powerful and intelligent of all beings, God, that he needed Woman to keep from being alone. God's first thoughts on women went like this: "Man, this is not a good thing. You are alone, really alone, with many animals to remind you that you exist as a lone man. I am going to make you someone who will be with you, made to enjoy this same place, not from another planet, or another species, but from you and for you."

The way we interpret God's ideas on this first Woman will guide us to answer some of the most essential questions about our identity, our purpose, and our soul. If we get this Woman wrong, if we get her beginning, her purpose, her role, and her giftings wrong, we will never reclaim God's image in women. We must wrestle with why this Woman was made and placed here on earth. We must wonder if she was meant to be a gift for Man, for earth, for God, or for all three.

Why Women's Studies Must Begin in Eden

The majority of scholars would say that Woman was made for Man. And in a way she was. She was his help, or *ezer* in Hebrew. *Ezer* reminds me of a certain Eben*ezer* Scrooge — a grouchy man who eventually grew into his name and became one who helped. I wonder though, is the name *ezer* big enough for women? Could the women in *Sex and the City* fit into it? What about Jessica Simpson? How about Hillary Clinton or Margaret Thatcher? Is it too narrow for them? What about Charlie's Angels? Can they squeeze into it? What about today's working woman? Is *ezer* too small for her? Is the name *ezer* something we understand, something we want to live with, something we eagerly claim?

If *ezer* is limiting, then God has limited us. If *ezer* is not limiting, then God has called us to an open, free, deep, and wide place.

The creation story in Genesis is not the only time Scripture uses *ezer*; it pops up several times. If we looked at these uses of *ezer*, our understanding of Eve — and of all women — may be enlarged, enhanced, and enlightened. We might see that God calls himself an *ezer*.

Ezer means deliverer, as in "The God of my father was my *ezer*, and delivered me from the sword of Pharaoh."[1]

Ezer means warrior: "Hear, O LORD, the voice of Judah, And bring him to his people. With his hands he contended for them, And may You be an *ezer* against his adversaries."[2]

Ezer means protection: "Blessed are you, O Israel; Who is like you, a people saved by the LORD, Who is the shield of your *ezer* And the sword of your majesty! So your enemies shall cringe before you, And you will tread upon their high places."[3]

Ezer means support: "May He send you *ezer* from the sanctuary and support you from Zion!"[4]

Ezer delivers the afflicted and needy: "But I am afflicted and needy; Hasten to me, O God! Thou are my *ezer* and my deliverer, O LORD, do not delay."[5]

Ezer means a shield: "You who fear the LORD, trust in the Lord; He is their *ezer* and their shield."[6]

Ezer is capable, vibrant help better than strong mountains: "I will lift up my eyes to the mountains; From where shall my *ezer* come? My *ezer* comes from the LORD, Who made heaven and earth."[7]

Ezer gives hope: "How blessed is he whose *ezer* is the God of Jacob, Whose hope is in the LORD his God."[8]

So although in Genesis 2, *ezer* is often translated "helper" or "helpmeet," its meaning includes far more. Woman is Man's *ezer*— she is a delivering, warring, supporting, shielding, capable, and vibrant female image bearer of God. What about putting those words in our Bible's margin to refresh our understanding of helper?

In Dr. Gray's book, you don't see women like this. Women for him are from another planet and are not made to interact with Martians. In most Christian literature, from novels to pop-culture devotionals, you don't see women like this. Women are fragile and secretarial, beautiful and at rest, submissive and quiet. And in the ancient Greek myth about Pandora, one girl's curiosity is the beginning of the world's problems. She opens a box full of malice, destruction, and death. The pestilence swarms out to begin the cycles of havoc and pain. Pandora's curiosity got the better of her and that's how, as Greek girls learned, evil came to the earth. You can blame the woman for evil in Greek, Jewish, and Christian creation stories. But perhaps we've spent too much time on the evil, less on the good that Woman was made to be.

The story of Eden begins before the fall and judgment. God's story gives us a rare, often overlooked snapshot of God creating femininity. Here, contrary to popular pagan myths, contrary to Goddess Earth myths, and contrary to much Churchianity, God makes Woman to provide and offer the hope, the *ezer* for Man. Woman brings the hope, the *ezer* for God as well. In his image, God made them, male and female.

God thought earth needed Woman, not for Man's laundry or for tending the children, as there weren't any kids to take care of or clothes to wash. And you'll notice when there are clothes to sew, it is a group project (Gen. 3:7). When she arrived, Woman provided more than companionship for Man, more than her uterus and breasts, more than a docile, sweet sexiness. She provided more of God's image on earth. As Catholic theologian Thomas Hopko points out, "Adam cannot be the 'image and glory of God' without Eve."[9] From this twoness we get the one picture: God's image on planet Earth.

We were made by God and brought to Man, but we were not made to be *used* by men — we were made for God, to be used for God's kingdom and destiny, along with Man. God thought Man and Woman should both be created in his image. God blessed both and thought both capable of receiving the command to subdue and take dominion.[10]

Women, we can relax. We are not second best. We are not afterthoughts, nor are we some lofty, perfect crown of creation. In terms of creation order, the last thing God made was marriage. The crown of his creation is the community of man and woman, being together. Women are not "mere helpers." We are not the correcting moralizers to fix those wild males. We have dominion to conquer whether we are married or not. We have work to undertake, whether we have children or not. We have *ezer* souls to share with God, man, and earth.

The great niece of Harriet Beecher Stowe was Charlotte Perkins Gilman, a suffragette and author who said that woman was designed to stand beside man as the "comrade of his soul, not the servant of his body."[11] Perhaps the arguments from her great aunt's *Uncle Tom's Cabin* encouraged Gilman to count women also as worthy of human rights. No matter what the Serpent said and continues to say, God created Woman who was sufficient to be co-laborer and co-dominion taker. She was made to think with Man, to feel with Man, to choose and introspect in stride with Man, to partner with Man's robust and strong soul because her own soul is also strong—strong enough to face the Enemy of our souls. Even after the curse, Woman's soul was no more pockmarked than Man's; the curse marked us differently, but that doesn't mean Woman was cut off from any of her capacities. As they trudged out of Eden, Woman and Man remained together.

Men and Women: More Similar Than Different

A problem has long afflicted Western society, both inside and outside the church. After the fall, people began to forget that Man and Woman were created to work together in harmony. Instead of focusing on all the ways that men and women are the same—both created in the image of God, and both created to bear the image of God in the world—people began to focus on all the ways we're different.

Essentialism, the idea that there is something essentially different about men and women, has hurt women more than it's helped us. Throughout history, most supposedly "natural" differences were anything but natural. For instance, telegraph operators were usually women because men thought females were "naturally" suited for the work. Females were made to be "more patient at being shut in a confined space" and "very good at spelling and writing neatly." Besides, "women are less likely than men to join together to protest about low wages."[12] From this list women are "naturally" unfidgety, patient, domestic, and meek.

Beyond refusing to give women the freedom to own property or hold on to their well-paying jobs after marriage, women were often denigrated as "naturally" incapable of hard thinking. Work in the academy, law, or medicine was beyond her abilities. Up until 1887, women were barred from Columbia's Law School on the basis that they "had not the mentality to study law."[13] Women were not trained to think because their bodies were "naturally" unfit for rigorous intellectual labor. Thinking might weaken women, or worse, drive them into madness. Without the physical constitution to endure higher education, it's no wonder women were believed to be unfit for casting votes.

Now, of course, women can study, teach, and even lead. Women are planning operations and devising strategies in virtually every industry, from heavy manufacturing, science, and computer technology to consumer products, fashion, and media.[14] And yet, there are some who doubt that a woman should be in these places. One can still find people who argue that a woman's "natural" sphere is internal, private, hidden just like our reproductive organs are hidden and internal, in spite of the fact that women's nature seems to handle the public strains quite well.

With women barred from research for most of the nineteenth century, it was easier for scientists to "prove" women's mental deficiencies. In 1879 scientists argued that women's brains were closer to "those of gorillas than to the most developed male brains."[15] Wasn't this evidence alone sufficient grounds for closing medical school to them? And yet this very same year, despite accusatory voices, the Massachusetts Medical Society threw open their doors to aspiring female doctors.[16]

Today, people continue to focus on the ways that science bolsters a theory of gender difference, instead of honoring the similarities between men and women. Too often in a conversation about gender difference, what is understood as "male" is considered better than what is considered "female." "Female" is the "opposite sex" or the "second sex." Male characteristics are considered normal, and female characteristics are said to be abnormal. Woman's difference, something that was supposed to show the world more of God, becomes deviation and deviation becomes sin. Women become the peculiar, inadequate humans. Even a good thing like some women remaining faithful church attendees is being called a problem, the church is "over-feminized."[17] Rather than holding the men responsible for their own slipped attendance or praising the women for faithfulness during a time when many Christian women are more pitied than respected for supporting Orthodoxy, femininity is called a problem.[18] But women were not always the problem. The original story doesn't fault Woman for weakness; in fact, in Eden the Scripture says that it was Man who had the need.

Equality for Women from Mary

We don't need to be discouraged by the poor scientific research from ages past. Nor do we need to feel overly threatened by neurological or hormonal research on the female brain. If we want to see how God values women, we only need look at something unique to the Christian story, where God finds one woman mentally and physically strong enough to bear his Son.

With the incarnation, we learn that God thought Mary a full-fledged part of humanity, enough so that she would provide all the human DNA strands for Jesus. In a culture that deified the phallus and honored males more than females, God gets counter-cultural and proves a woman's body and soul is all that his Son needs for his humanity.[19] Not to ignore the Holy Spirit's overshadowing, Mary was the first human participant in the miracle of God becoming flesh. Jesus would claim his human heritage from a female. This means that women must be as human as men, as capable of bearing God's image as men. Christ inherited all his human abilities to think, choose, feel, and desire from his mother.

The incarnation also puts Jesus in a place to redeem women. God thought men and women similar enough that a male sacrifice could propitiate for a female soul. The temple system had prepared the Jews for such a possibility—for thousands of years, male goats and lambs and bulls shed their blood for women's sins, so maybe no one thought twice about it. But for me, a female Gentile living in the twenty-first century, who has not experienced years of bringing a male animal to the temple, it is stunning. It amazes me unless I believe men and women are similar enough that a Man could cover all female and male sins.

Jesus died once for all, his propitiation making a resounding argument for the similarity of men and women. One man's body and soul redeemed all women's bodies and souls. When the Father accepted the male Jesus as a sufficient sacrifice to redeem both sexes, he was also saying men and women are not so polarized or irreconcilable to be in a never-ending gender war. That is precisely what Paul says, the wall has been broken, the veil is torn, there is neither male nor female, we are all one in Christ.[20]

Having grown up and schooled myself in the inherent superiority of men, it is vital for me to remember that it was not Jesus's masculinity that made him pleasing to the Father. His masculinity was expected and foretold, but on the cross it was Christ's humanity and divinity that counted for us.

Science Supports Eden

Some of the most rigorous psychological research shows that men and women are quite similar. As professor Robert Nadeau put it, "In virtually all computer-based studies on the mental abilities of men and women, what is most significant is the amazing degree of overlap."[21] Instead of feeling worried that secular psychologists and scientists are destroying gender roles, perhaps we should take comfort in knowing that men and women are quite similar. This doesn't mean that men and women are identical, nor that we are interchangeable parts. You can be equal without being identical. It is Eden's teaching that men and women are made as human souls; we share our humanity so we should be prepared to find more evidence of our similarity than evidence to the contrary.

Dr. Janet Shibley Hyde, a psychologist at the University of Wisconsin, has compiled a summary of thousands of psychological gender studies.[22] Her meta-analysis blows the whistle on much of the sensational research that passes for "proof" of substantial gender difference. Back in the 1980s her work represented a summary of the verbal abilities of 1,418,899 people. Two decades later Hyde updated and expanded this cumulative study, providing another several-page-long table that shows no gender differences in some of the places we'd most expect: verbal skills, vocabulary, writing, anagrams, and reading comprehension. In 2005 Hyde published her most recent research in one of the most widely respected and read psychological peer-reviewed journals, *American Psychologist*.[23] Her work offers the collaborated effort of hundreds of research psychologists, people whose job it is to dive deeper than the anecdotal, clinical experience of psychologists like Dr. Gray.

From her collaborations, Hyde has found sufficient evidence to suggest replacing the differences model with a Gender Similarity Hypothesis, which states that while men and women are not identical, they aren't all that different. In other words, our differences shrink in comparison to our similarities.

Most gender studies specifically look at the areas we assume men and women differ, things like verbal skills,[24] visual-spatial ability,[25] mathematical ability,[26] and aggression.[27] Comparing these areas, Hyde found that the difference is slight. Men and women don't, in fact, differ very much, even in areas of presumed, stereotypical difference. Hyde is not claiming men and women are identical — she notes that there are some differences; women smile more when they're being watched than men, men masturbate more than women, women do not approve of casual sex as much as men. But these differences are often degreed, depending on each person. The way all women differ from all men is less predictive, provocative, and universal than we might think.

The gap between women and men is more like the following graph (Gender Similarity):

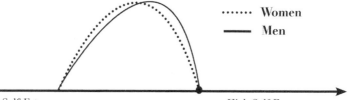

We are similar though not the same. In statistical terms, 85 percent of the area overlaps. I wish I had heard that in my geometry class, or even in my youth group. The difference is actually so slight, that knowing a person's gender has little to no predictive power in nearly 80 percent of psychological matters.[28] And indeed, areas of difference, such as self-esteem (men, unsurprisingly, tend to have higher self-esteem than women), may be due to family culture, environment, or personality, not to an essential difference in our souls.

Books written by clinical (not research) psychologists often make too much of smaller studies or personal stories that indicate some gender differences. These are not collaborated studies, but anecdotal observations from their clinical work (a much smaller sampling of the population). They end up making men and women look more different than similar. But these studies must exaggerate the general findings to do it, so that similarities end up looking like the graph on page 74.

We just can't gobble down any perceived differences because we want to find them. If we notice a few women prefer romance movies while most men prefer violent flicks, we cannot then generalize from this observation that women are made to relate and men are designed to be ready for battle.[29] This is to marvel and focus on a difference

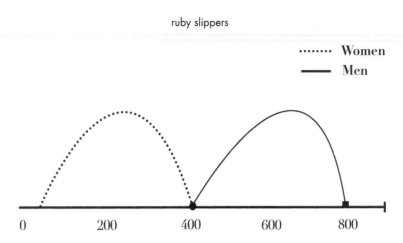

in movie preference, forgetting the scores of men who want deep and meaningful relationships and women whose violence of choice is alive and well; we just call it passive aggression.

It's difficult not to notice these little disparities between some men and women; I find the differences fascinating. Mars/Venus mythology has tapped into the otherness that we enjoy about the other sex. I find the different men in my life as interesting and mysterious as they find women. What is mysterious begs our attention to figure out. But this doesn't mean either sex must always be a mystery or that we are vastly different. For most examples of femininity and masculinity, there are examples to the contrary, which means the definition is wanting.

My eagerness to find difference often leads me to believe things before I have enough evidence. This is where our will and beliefs must come into play. How determined are you, right now, to believe that men and women are incredibly different? How hopeful or worried are you in finding we are similar? And regardless of how invested you are in finding a difference, let's make a commitment to resist the urge to stereotype, especially if we personally know men and women who are living examples to the contrary.

When I first read Hyde's research, I was surprised and a tad unsettled, and then I began to feel like pieces that had never fit before suddenly were falling into place. As will become clear throughout this book, I do believe that women are different from men. And yet, I have come to realize that if we are going to talk meaningfully about gender difference, we need cumulative research like Hyde's. We need to know about the distinctive characteristics that all women — not just women in my Orange County church or North American Christian culture — share. I want to be able to line up my ideas with reality, not exaggerated graphs. I want to improve my communication with my male friends, my father, my brother, and especially my husband, but not at the cost of agreeing with uncollaborated, sensational, embellished differences. That doesn't honor men or women, and it certainly doesn't honor God.

Mars and Venus Mythology in the Church

Research like Hyde's, demonstrating the large overlap of similarities between men and women, can be unsettling because our assumptions about gender differences run so deep. Even those of us who think we have shed our gender biases often hold on to some deep-seated notions about the differences between men and women. Just think: how do you react when you meet a female mathematician or a woman philosopher? How about when you encounter a woman who is confident, independent, secure, single, childless, and self-fulfilled? How do you react to women who don't want to have children or prefer talking politics over child-rearing? How do you react to the woman who prefers cycling to scrapbooking? Are you surprised? Suspicious that the confident biker philosophy queen has something to prove or hide?

Several months ago my monthly book club was baffled over Alexander McCall Smith's convincing development of his female protagonist, Mma Ramotswe, in *The No. 1 Ladies Detective Agency*. Most of the group — women and men — demanded to know how a man could write such a convincing woman, and wondered why Smith hadn't chosen a male protagonist. Is it a feat for a novelist to create convincing characters of the opposite sex, when Dorothy L. Sayers understands Lord Peter Wimsey or a Henry James writes *A Portrait of a Lady*? When I voiced my idea that perhaps it's not so shocking a feat since men and women are not hugely different, some in our book club laughed at me. The rest sat in surprised silence.

The Mars-versus-Venus mythology is accepted as the norm. We can hear it at coffee houses, at playgrounds, and in marriage fellowship groups. I regularly find assumptions about total, radical gender difference lurking in the glossy bulletin pages of American church life. Consider the women's and men's ministries I read about while recently visiting a church in Orange County. On pastel pink letterhead, the women's ministry explained it was a group that would teach women to "walk with Jesus." Women would be inspired to "fall deeply in love with Jesus." This sounded good to me, even though I'm not a fan of "falling in love" language. Then I noticed the blue handout for the men. The men's ministry wanted to "build mature men in Christ" by developing "strong believers" with knowledge in order to "reproduce the character of Christ" for the purpose of glorifying God in every aspect of their lives. In the end, these are the same goals, but the way they are communicated says that the women's group will be relational and emotional and the men's group will be about strength and character.

To back up these assumptions about gender, churches often quote Ephesians 5:22–25. The teaching goes like this: God commands men and women to do the things that are most difficult for us. Besides a sort of sadistic version of God's love, this communicates that women are naturally loving, which is why women aren't commanded to love, but to respect. Men, however, aren't as naturally loving, which is why God must command them to love their wives. Endless convoluted ideas about manhood and womanhood grow from this strange interpretation of love and respect. Are women better than men at loving?

And if women are loving their husbands already, ergo the absence of "love your husbands," why does Paul underscore their need to respect their husbands? Can we really love someone without respecting them? Are men so emotionally stagnant that they need to be commanded to love? Is this passage even talking about gender theory at all?

I have a hard time imagining love being divorced from respect. Why can't love and respect be two sides of the same coin, a coin that is the currency of all relationships? Paul doesn't separate the two when he tells the older women to "encourage the young women to love their husbands, . . . to be sensible."[30] Ah, yes, sensible. I can't see how God is honored when we squeeze out a universal gender theory from a command to married people in Ephesus. It fails to incorporate widows and widowers, unmarried college students, young girls and boys, all of whom are male and female image bearers of God. A comprehensive and useful gender theory must include all of us.

When books announce without scriptural or psychological or theological evidence that men give love to get sex and women give sex to get love, that women are more emotionally than physically needy, that men are not relational, I want to meet with the authors and tell them that it isn't like that in my life, and it wasn't like that in the early church. In Corinth it was the widows who burned with passion, which is why Paul exhorted them to marry.[31] Yes, widows!

Devotional books for women often present exaggerated gender differences and shopworn anecdotes as proof of God's ideas of femininity or masculinity. They do it without citation, without collaboration, and without justification. And I am rather weary of it. The church is perhaps more eager to find sex *differences* than to honor the human *similarities. Ransomed Heart Ministries* or *The Journal for Biblical Manhood and Womanhood* is no more immune than *National Geographic.*[32]

Mars and Venus mythology perpetuates a harmful version of essentialism, one that sticks women into corsets and men into armor.

Gender stereotypes hurt both sexes, relegating women into the private, softer sphere, barring the Marys from learning at Jesus's feet, in the name of protecting them from the "real world" of theology, commerce, and politics. Stereotyping the sexes forces men into emotional constipation and excuses them from relational community. Community, the very thing God knew Man needed in making Woman.

Gender stereotypes justify our assumptions that if we know a person's gender, we know all we need to know about them. It's another way to excuse us from seeing the variety in God's image on earth. It's not a harmless mistake. All this gender shorthand ends up muting female image bearers. To exclude women from using a gift she has—or to encourage women to exercise their gifts but then never provide institutional space for them to do so—offers her the cake (you are equal before God), but snatches it away when she trustingly picks up a fork to dig in.

Created Equal

The glimmer of hope is the soul. Our souls prove that we are not so different. We are all human with human capacities, whether we're actualizing them or not, whether our brains are small or large. This is what gives us admittance into the human species—not our size, not our age, not our gender, not our function, not our usefulness, but our human souls. The soul, with all its capacities, is the cornerstone for our belief in the equality of all people of all ages and colors. And, yes, even the woman's soul.

Soul Care

1. Adam was made first. Does that bother you? Does it sound like man was made "ahead of" Eve, and somehow won first place? Journal your ideas about "first" being better. Where did they come from?

2. Do you like the word "helper"? What does it make you think about? How does the description of God being *ezer* change your beliefs about helpers?

3. See Genesis 49:25; Exodus 18:4; Deuteronomy 33:7, 26, 29; 1 Samuel 7:12; and Psalms 20:2; 33:20. What characteristics does an *ezer* need to have? Do you want to grow your soul into *ezer-hood*? Why or why not?

4. When you hear a joke about gender stereotypes, do you laugh over it? If not, why not?

5. Ask yourself if you are fully comfortable with your femininity and then sit in silence for ten minutes. Journal your thoughts. As one professor told me, "Few have grasped the meaning of their gender unless they have wrestled with it."

6. How have you propagated exaggerated differences between men and women? What do you do with the exceptions to your rule?

7. Think about what you uniquely contribute to your male friends. Journal a list of character qualities that you consider to be unique strengths of women.

8. Do you think the fall changed the soul of Woman? If so, how?

four

leaving eden

Prairie Muffins do not reflect badly on their husbands
by neglecting their appearance; they work with the clay
God has given, molding it into an attractive package for
the pleasure of their husbands, they own aprons and know how
to use them, they place their husbands' needs and desires above
other obligations, arranging their schedules and responsibilities
so that they do not neglect the one who provides for
and protects them and their children.

Prairie Muffin Manifesto[1]

I was in seminary on September 11, 2001, sitting in a lecture hall dominated by soon-to-be pastors and philosophers. We all listened in stunned silence as we learned that the second tower of the World Trade Center had collapsed. In the wake of the news, one student put his hand up. He was a little older than me, a surfer with bleached, spiked hair and strong shoulders.

"We know who did this," he said, his face unnaturally red, his hands twitching in agitation on the desk. "Why is the United States just sitting around? We need to do something." Then he said what I think he wanted to say all along: "What keeps us from just nuking the Arabs?"

I raised my eyebrows in protest. The men around me were nodding, making those rumbling agreement sounds, rustling their hands in eagerness.

Eagerness for what? Did they really think they could implement justice? I was in the middle of a *Christian seminary*, and yet I was surrounded by bloodthirsty men, men who just last week were working on sermons about loving our neighbors as ourselves. Now they wanted someone's head on a platter.

I wanted out of there. I looked at the only other woman in the class. Her brows furrowed, her eyes darted around the room. I leaned over to my fiancé and whispered, "They don't know who did this!" Without looking at me, Dale said, "They're angry."

It was then that I felt how different men were. I was beginning to believe Martian men mythology. But as I think back to that time, it really would have been a shallow conversion experience. It wasn't fair to construct my gender theory based on this event. This was not men at their best. Men are not essentially vengeful, hotheaded, angry, and reactive, while women are careful, compassionate, clear-headed, and wise.

It was a bad time to judge. That is the rub, isn't it? Is there ever a good time to judge men and women, a picture-perfect moment to capture our essence? Is there ever a good time to distinguish how men and women "really" are?

Piecing Together Femininity

Besides a spell of paradise in Eden and the exquisite life of Jesus, there are no intact, human specimens, no illustrative, inspiring guides to show us what men and women should look like. And since Adam, Eve, and Jesus never underwent extensive psychological evaluation, we are left a bit puzzled about the goal or natural state of human beings. What is our goal? What should humans be? What should our souls look like? How are male and female image bearers supposed to be different?

Theologians have worked to put together the picture. Jesus is like the picture on top of a puzzle box, something to guide us as we gather the corner pieces and organize the colors. But we end up finding a lot of pieces in our souls that don't seem to look anything like Jesus. Where do those pieces go? In our shame, we end up hiding them.

Human nature, once whole, is now cracked, like an exquisite glass vase with a splinter right down the center. The crack ruins the dignity and usefulness of the vase. The crack ruins our beauty, and instead of being perfect bearers of God's image, we too often exhibit all that God is not. As one sexually abused female in the church writes, "Underneath everything ... even these words, there is woundedness that has no description. There is fundamental damage, a crack in the foundation."[2]

We are the only created beings that choose against our nature. Rocks fall, birds fly, but humans don't obey the laws that God gave us for human flourishing. We don't obey the laws of reality, the laws hinted at in the Ten Commandments, the laws of wisdom that say if you're married, don't flirt with other men, because while it might feel exciting for one night, you'll make the ones you really love miserable afterward; the laws that say love your friend who betrayed you, even though it hurts and you want to close up, love her for your sake as much as hers. As *The Book of Common Prayer* puts it, "We have left undone those things which we ought to have done; and we have done those things which we ought not to have done." We are cracked mirrors who don't reflect the human image of God back to him.

If God operated like a CEO, he might order a recall on us because of the defect in our core operating system.[3] Our souls are dysfunctional. Our souls are warped so that we actually want to act against our nature. We want to eat donuts all morning, we want to sit in front of the fifth hour of reruns, we want to leave the ones we love, we want to hide, we want to lie and lust, envy and despise. We are torn, reason doesn't hold sway anymore, our emotions are not well-ordered much less well-understood, our desires are weak, our compass doesn't point north.[4] The damage runs straight through our core, like the cracked vase. We can't judge our nature based on warped examples. We can't judge the nature of women unless we know a perfect woman. If we could interview Eve, we might discover her nature before she and Adam tweaked it, and that would be grand. Instead, what we have is the witness of Scripture, and the shattered image in us and in women around us to look at, to figure out what woman should be.

The crack runs deep. Man and woman's capacity to take dominion together was damaged. Our bodies, meant to move with grace and control, are slowed by disease and arthritis. We are living out the last part of the curse, for dust we are and to dust we will return. We live out the middle of the curse; instead of working together, woman desires more from man, man rules more than woman, earth bucks man's hand, and children pain their mothers. And this is our home, east of Eden. With our ruined natures, we live and love.

Femininity has been broken. We have the Evil One to battle. In *The Wizard of Oz*, the witch works her own public relations campaign to tarnish Dorothy's reputation. By the time Dorothy gets to the Emerald City, she's not just Dorothy from Kansas; she's become "the witch's Dorothy." Our femininity has also been renamed by the Father of Lies. He keeps right on twisting the warrior-like *ezer* of Eden into something weak, fearful, and inconsequential. Femininity no longer seems a badge of honor, pointing to our Maker. To some women, it's not even worth redeeming; they'd like to get rid of the word altogether.

When Eve chose to leave Eden—and yes, she did choose—she walked out with a shattered image. She was less than she was meant to be, not because she was naturally frail, but because she chose to leave the Source and Maker of life. Away from God, she learned what it means to become irritable, deceitful, demanding, manipulative, faithless, and cold.

God can mend this broken image. He can redeem us, our bodies, our souls, our lives. He is the master at remaking his shattered cameos of earth. But it's difficult to accept his mending if we don't even think we're broken. We are the only ones who can hand him the pieces.

Becoming More Natural, Becoming More Human

To say "nature" means to inquire about something's design.[5] The nature of hearts is to pump blood. Eve's nature is the way God designed women to be. Knowing Eve's nature helps us know woman's designated purpose — we will better know what it is Christ wants to redeem.

We have what we need to be like God, souls made in his image. Like a bud, we begin to show what we have within. What was always there — the red slippers, the full-blooded, robust femininity — buds into full bloom. We can become fully feminine, and fully human.[6]

Because we live east of Eden, our image-bearing is a gift and a task, our "humanity is both present in reality and a goal to reach."[7] We have not obtained this full image, yet.[8] God became human so we might become conformed to the image of his Son.[9] Paul says it like this: "We all ... are being transformed into the same image from glory to glory, just as from the Lord, the Spirit."[10]

Souls East of Eden

Adam and Eve both left the garden. Eve, tempted by forbidden fruit, set up her own rules. She did so for good reasons, which is why she is called deceived — the wrong thing, for the right reason.

"You know, that fruit certainly looks perfect. It's almost a waste to let it just sit there, untouched, untasted, uncultivated, unenjoyed. It might make me wiser. It might give me power to be a better *ezer*, which is what God wants. Then I'll be a goddess, knowing good from evil." She plucks. "It can't hurt me if it will help me help him, help God, help this earth."

Moses wrote that she was deceived. She thought the fruit would do something it wouldn't. And she plucked and ate. It was the eating, not the initiating, that was a sin. It was wrong to give in to the Enemy instead of battling against the lie with her partner, Man.

When Adam ate, he chose to listen to an idea he *knew* was wrong.[11] And that was sin.

That the sin involved eating helps us picture the total spread of pollution in Adam and Eve's bodies and souls—like a poison being digested and then working through a person's body, their sin pervaded every aspect of their being. One blind Puritan spent years trying to describe this in *Paradise Lost*. John Milton explains that Adam and Eve's choice corrupted every soul capacity. Their emotions (Milton calls this capacity the appetite) claimed dominion in their souls, rather than playing the proper role as servant.

> *For Understanding ruled not, and the Will*
> *Heard not her lore, both in subjection now*
> *To sensual Appetite, who from beneath*
> *Usurping over sovereign Reason claimed*
> *Superior sway.*[12]

The "false Fruit" inflamed his carnal desires and Adam looked with "lascivious Eyes" on Eve.[13] And she returned that look with contagious fire. Adam and Eve, in Milton's version, burned with lust for each other. Adam looked at the flesh of his flesh and wanted her body alone, not her soul with it. It was the first raping and pillaging, not just Man of Woman, but Woman of Man. They took their dominion and turned it into domination. Natalie Imbruglia echoes this in her song "Torn." I wonder if this is how Eve felt the morning after.

> *I'm cold and I am shamed,*
> *Lying naked on the floor.*[14]

I think it's interesting that Adam and Eve together sewed their coverings. Not merely because Adam did some sewing, but because they hid, first from one another, and then from God. They must have felt awash in a new emotion, the guilt that we learn to manage every day. It must have been a pungent, memorable experience, something they might have talked about as the first tangible sense of their sin. The guilt that grows in us started right there in Eden. How painful those hours of waiting must have been, waiting in a shadowy grove where the guilty pair hid together and yet alone.

Their souls were warped. They left the *shalom* of Eden and lived as ruined souls, every capacity a bit tweaked, every belief tinged with lies, every emotion tainted by unruliness, every good desire becoming a struggle to strengthen, their spirits regularly in denial or hiding. We live their judgment. Thousands of years later, with science and knowledge growing, we still need that second Adam who prayed in another garden to pull us out of the judgment of Eden.

Different Judgments for Different Souls

It is merciful for God to come looking, for his judgment brings relief and clarity. As one preaching elder in my church said, "Guilt is not a long-term strategy with God." The Hound of Heaven, as Francis Thompson's poem explains, will come looking. God is on a no-holds-barred, long-term search for us. Judgment is the painful gouging and prying to get us out of the shadows to stand in his cleansing light. It hurts, but it isn't as wretched as life with never-ending guilt and shame. Standing in the Light begins the process of reconciliation, even though it feels worse at first.

Both Man and Woman's decision alienated them from God and estranged them from their true natures. Both would receive the judgment that one day their bodies would unravel from their souls. But the specific details of Man and Woman's judgments were different. Man's work changed: he would no longer enjoy sweat-free labor, the good, fulfilling work of Eden. And Woman's desire changed: her healthy desire for partnership was turned either too hot or too cold. Her desire could look like clingy neediness or coldhearted manipulation. And her partner, Man, would feel the repercussions of living with her. He would also feel pain in his work, and she would cry in pain while giving birth.

Why were Man and Woman given different punishments? Was it because each took the fruit for different reasons? Was it because their bodies were made differently? Was it because they had different souls? Maybe God had his own private reasons for judging them differently. If there had been any soul differences between Man and Woman before the judgment, these differences were magnified afterward.

In judging and cursing Woman separately from Man, I think there is also, ironically, a measure of dignity that God gifts to all women. He is saying she sinned uniquely, separately, willfully, so she fully deserved a separate judgment. God honors Woman as a separate, responsible human. God judges her capable of receiving and bearing this condemnation and carrying it in her body and soul. Even in the curse, God dignifies Woman with her own, customized judgment. Several chapters later in Genesis, the women fade into the background and it seems like the men alone are responsible.[15] But that's not what God thinks in Eden. He judges them both.

In judging Woman, God changes her desires, her power, and her life-producing freedom and ease. Her desire was now going to be different, intensely directed to her husband. It makes me wonder what her desire was like before. Had Man's desire been directed toward Woman in equal intensity? Had Woman's desire, before her sin, been more clearly focused on God? Would Man and Woman now experience desire that was ... imbalanced? Somehow this new desire was different. And now, Woman, who once partnered with Man in tasks like subduing, filling, and dominion taking together, was changed: "[Your husband] will rule over you." No more working together in mutual give-and-take, pain in childbearing would cut her off from working with him side by side. Pain would enter her life as she bore life: "In pain you will bring forth children."[16] Woman's curse affected

Man, of course. Woman's loss of power or dominion gave Man more dominion. The judgment of God, not the created order in Eden, delivered Woman into the hands of Man's domination.

With a flaming sword at their back forcing them out, Man and Woman left. Communion and dominion had dissolved into domination. They left Eden together, but with different scars. They would still live on the same planet, but life would be full of unfulfilled desires and pain in work and in birth. Woman was called Eve, the first dominion taking of man, now Adam, over his one-time partner. She is given her name by him.[17]

Living the Judgment

Here we live, east of Eden. We cannot subdue and steward the earth; we watch as volcanoes and earthquakes, hurricanes and tsunamis, overwhelm our lives. With minimized powers on earth, we plunder the earth and the people in it. We use the same God-given power to subdue and dominate each other. In the name of desire, women enable their men. And in the name of submission, men silence women, and women silence themselves. It's like there's a lie echoing in our souls, "We tried once to help and we failed, better to just give up trying. He can do it better, anyway." It reminds me of the Wicked Witch's words to Dorothy, "Give me back my slippers! I'm the only one that knows how to use them." And we surrender, thinking this is godly submission. Haven't we too quickly given up gifts that belong to us, deceived that others know better how to use and instruct us on our femininity?

It appears that Eden is forgotten. Western literature is filled with indications that we think our current state of affairs is permanent. The Greek Xenophon wrote, "It seems to me that God adapted women's nature to be indoor and man's to outdoor work ... as Nature has entrusted woman with ... *a timid nature*."[18] He doesn't think Woman was made to garden and cultivate the earth, like in Eden. The

Roman Cicero wrote, "Because of *women's weak judgment*, our ancestors wanted them to be subject to guardians."[19] Plato said women are weak, secretive, and crafty.[20] Demosthenes of Greece thought women were just cogs in the happiness machine for men: "Mistresses we keep for pleasure, concubines for daily attendance upon our person, wives to bear us legitimate children and be our faithful housekeepers."[21] These ideas come thousands, if not tens of thousands of years after Eden. These men were educated, intelligent, refined leaders of sophisticated societies that had conquered the world with Greek ideas and Roman armies.

Thousands of years after the judgment, man's domination is still apparent. Freud said that woman is a damaged reflection of man.[22] Pop spiritualist Dan Brown offers a boutique form of gnosticism and neo-paganism, reducing the feminine to a womb, a vagina, a sexual encounter. He canonizes the sexual gifts of females rather than dignifying the image-bearing soul capacities in women.[23] His femininity glories fertile, female bodies over female souls.

Throughout the centuries, the Christian church hasn't helped women carve out a place of dignity. Women are rarely considered full citizens, worthy of political or legal rights. And seldom are we permitted to be leaders, in church or in civil society. Though the Scriptures never say men are superior to women, the early church fathers interpreted some passages to mean just that. Augustine thought the best thing a woman could offer a man was her reproductive equipment. I know men who believe the same today.

The church encouraged the most holy men, the celibate monks and priests, to keep themselves unsullied by knowing a woman so intimately. Woman was considered a hindrance, not a help in knowing God.

According to Augustine, Eve was weak before the judgment. (And as much as I like John Milton, his Eve also seems prone to narcissism and weak thinking.) Eve obviously couldn't work the land as well as

Adam. Indeed, Augustine goes so far as to suggest that another man would have been a much more "suitable helper" for farming than a woman. He doesn't even entertain the idea that women's bodies may have been stronger before the fall.

Augustine thought Eve wasn't made to be a companion to Adam either: "For company and conversation, how much more agreeable it is for two male friends to dwell together than for a man and a woman!... I cannot think of any reason for woman's being made as man's helper; if we dismiss the reason of procreation."[24]

Augustine didn't believe a woman could image God as fully and completely as he or other men.[25]

While there are some glimmering moments along the church's history (the Protestant Reformation, for instance, brought out "the priesthood of all believers" providing justification for women to read and understand the Bible, Puritans began instructing females in doctrine and writing tracts, Quakers provided places for women to teach and preach), most of the church has frowned on women acting as full-bodied, full-souled images of God. The message that has been drummed into our minds is that something is inadequate in our being; somehow we don't make the final cut of image bearer of God. Somehow we are more polluted by the curse, so we live in an attempt to cover these scars from Eden.

When "gentle and quiet spirit" becomes merely modest clothing, purity before marriage, and anti-assertive personalities, we see how womanhood becomes about covering and holding back.[26] When women are told that femininity is ruining the church, they start to wonder if it's their fault. Men are still exercising dominion over women. How many women have been asked to wrestle with the commands addressed to women, the real meaning of "gentle and quiet spirit"? How free are we to be honest and transparent as we share our thoughts on Christian womanhood?

When women choose the church norms of femininity instead of wondering if Christ wants us to grow deeper to understand our womanhood, we muffle God's image in ourselves. When we toe the party line instead of questioning, wondering, and doubting the script we've been given, we allow our desire for a husband or the men we admire to rule even our own souls. We are living the curse.

But we are living it with "feminine" frills. We have pink witness-wear, dainty cross jewelry, and flowery bookmarks. We can buy embroidered Bible covers and go to women's Bible studies, which are geared to help us accept our curse. Some of these women's Bible study groups give us more lists, ways to be more gentle, quiet, and submissive. It is easy to take the medicine, the prescribed formula for femininity. We are told that we really are happier when a man takes care of us. That we feel safer that way. That we are natural followers. And the studies we read, the jobs we accept, the pay we earn, all testify to our belief that this subordination is true femininity. It's much simpler to settle and forget about the ruby slippers. It's simpler, and anyway, isn't this just the way life is? Isn't this God's judgment on us?

Free to Be Fierce?

No wonder there were women who tried to change things a bit. In the 1970s women broadened their shoulders, slapped on slacks, and got down and dirty in the marketplace. Some women denied there was a male or female nature and ended up trying to act like fallen males. They were following the words of one of the first secular feminists, Mary Wollstonecraft, who wanted women to become "more masculine and respectable."[27] Women parroted men's vices, proving just how competitive, ruthless, and promiscuous they could be.[28]

By attempting to completely obliterate the differences between the sexes, women conformed to modern male standards of efficiency and success. Women took a male form—a fallen male form—and called it secular feminism, a belief system that supposedly elevated the power of woman.[29] But it did more damage to both sexes in the process.

You can see it all over our culture. In Hollywood, women are as racy, seductive, competitive, and vengeful as the men. They just compete in heels, mini-skirts, and black leather. In the business world women show they can be as demanding, controlling, and manipulative as men, with their sassy business suits and their styled hair, showing more cleavage and leg as signs of their power.

My grandmother—who grew up in the 1940s, married in the 1950s, raised teenagers in the 1960s, and reinvented herself as a business woman in the 1970s—cannot stand the word *feminine*. She grimaces and tells me, "It reminds me of feminine products." But femininity is more than menstruation, babies, and nursing. It is more than the "feminine products" dispensers in women's bathrooms. It is more than beauty, fashion, and svelte figures. It is more than coy flirting, batted eyes, soft skin, bubble baths, and sugar and spice. It is more than the purse-toting, bauble-flashing, provocative behavior, and mincing steps of supermodels and drag queens. It requires more than a sex change to be feminine.[30] It means more than style and haircuts that are sassy enough to catch some boy's eye.

Femininity is more than becoming like a man; it is also more than becoming like most church-sanctioned models of womanhood.

Frivolous, Flimsy, and Flawed Views of "Femininity"

We don't want the skimpy femininity, the helper without the Godlike image, the perfect Christian woman whose very perfection keeps her on a pedestal. That is femininity lite. She might look good, she might draw the attention of important elders, decision makers, and CEOs, but this femininity won't pierce our souls. It will only be something we do, not something we are. It won't be the original ruby slippers that God gave us.

Femininity isn't the caring, submissive, sensitive, emotional, passive, modest, slim, Bible-studying woman that the church promotes. None of these taken individually or together is a distinctly feminine characteristic. These are all human characteristics, and I know men who embody them all. Men are caring (they hurt when we berate them for missing that exit, again; they care about our opinion of them). Men are emotional (crying isn't more feminine nor is sharing your emotions or caring about relationships; when Dale plans our anniversary or writes a poem, he is not being naturally feminine, he is being human). Men are submissive (they submit to God, to their boss, to the IRS, to you, if they believe 1 Corinthians 7:4). Men are prayerful (look at King David's prayer book in the Psalms). Men are sensitive (especially if you tell them your expectations ahead of time). Men are slim (trim, lean, and muscular is the ideal for both sexes). Men are modest (I wish more would be so—I've seen enough boxers spilling out of the top of sagging jeans to last me a lifetime). And men go to Bible studies. This list is good for all people, not just for women. And it's certainly not a measure of our femininity.

"Feminine" comes up conspicuously in the fashion industry quite a bit, so it's easy to think femininity is mainly about our style. One girl explained to me after a talk I gave that she wishes her friends would be more feminine. When I asked her to clarify, she said, "You know, they need to feel comfortable wearing skirts and makeup." Now perhaps they would enjoy a fashion change, perhaps it might be linked to growing their feminine soul as we will talk about later, but fashion changes are not always an indication of our femininity. A magazine may highlight a "feminine frilly skirt" or "feminine pumps" or "feminine scarves," but femininity isn't about the lace and corset ties and padding that Victoria's Secret markets. If dress made females feminine, then some cross-dressers and drag queens are more feminine than I am with a ponytail, sweats, and a sports bra. We don't want the look, we want the real, natural feminine soul.

Nor must one be beautiful to be feminine. I know the world demands beauty out of women — that isn't even debatable. But a better question is, "Should women feel responsible to give our beauty the way the world wants it?"

I find it fascinating that Jesus never talks about a woman providing the world with beauty. Jesus never even comments on a woman's beauty, though he regularly asks women to contribute their souls.[31] The triune God never says Eve was made for beauty. On the contrary, both humans were made to work, to love each other, and to glorify God.

We don't need women to provide all the beauty for the world. Men are beautiful too — check out an Abercrombie and Fitch store, Michelangelo's *David*, or even Absalom in the Bible: "Now in all Israel was no one as handsome as Absalom, so highly praised; from the sole of his foot to the crown of his head there was no defect in him."[32] Beauty is not a unique possession of women, nor is it the core of femininity. If the world can only find beauty in a woman, then they are only seeing a sliver of God's beauty.[33] Beauty is all around. I see it in my pack of three Corgi puppies tearing up and down the garden path, stumbling over each other in a heap of fluffy hair to greet me. I see it in baby Linus's face when he laughs. I see it in my husband's poems to me. I see it in a shiny apple. I see it in Grace in *Dogville*. I see it in Christ in *The Passion*.

Accepting the stereotypical feminine stuff is much easier, I'll grant that. Accepting the prescribed role is much safer, but we do not follow a safe God. Our God requires more of us than that.

Natural Femininity

I will sometimes sigh in a moment of loneliness and run to ask Dale for a listening ear. He listens, he loves, and he holds me. And I am comforted. But even after his care, I have caught myself saying, "I really want to talk to a girlfriend right now." And I call up Jodi or Erin, and they listen to me. And I am comforted, again, but in another way.

One of the groundbreaking thinkers on womanhood and co-parenthood is Christian sociologist Mary Stewart Van Leeuwen.[34] In her book *Gender and Grace*, she reminds both genders of the one need that God put into our souls, our need for each other. Eden means somehow, someway, under all the plumage, heels, and makeup, women need men. And somehow, under all the ties and pressed shirts, greasy coveralls, and macho veneer, men need women. Van Leeuwen writes:

> I believe that, at its best and undistorted by sin (and these are of course huge qualifiers) the constant invention and reinvention of gender roles is an expression of our creation-based sense that women and men need each other. Thus we search for ways to symbolize that need ... much like a sacrament ... the observance of gender roles and rituals reminds us that men and women are incomplete without each other. But sacraments, like everything else, can be abused.[35]

Too often, our roles become legalistic. Instead of flexible postures or suggested dancing steps, they harden into a stone coffin, chiseled to fit only one shape. And we can't budge to ask or wonder or imagine any differently. Women who want to be loved more than they want truth will live in this tomb. We will accept the role and ignore the signs that we are stifled and uncomfortable. We forget about the door slamming, the keys locking us in because we're so gleeful about being accepted in church, at school, in the women's Bible study, at home, and — we think — in heaven, too.

The word "role" itself sounds contrived. It smacks of my high school plays, where someone tells me what to say, when, and how to say it. Something like, *Enter wife stage left, carrying steaming cinnamon rolls.* I love making cinnamon rolls, but I make them because I want to, because I'm the best cook in my house, not because I've been instructed to do so. It is an artful and free exercise of my love.

Roles lack two essential ingredients: flexibility and honesty. In trying to define natural femininity, it's really important that we don't make it a role; it must be about something we are, not merely what we act like. If I cannot find femininity in my soul, if I can only find it in a select group of women, say Christians who attend church regularly, then femininity is not an essential part of me; it is only a role I play. As Eugene Peterson, long-time pastor and writer says, all people are free to "live a life that spills out of the stereotyped containers that a sin-inhibited society provides."[36] But women, especially Christian women, don't often feel free to see how God might be more honored and glorified if they spill out of their assigned role.

If our souls are feminine, then our nature is permanently and essentially and naturally feminine. This is what philosophers call an ontological or essential difference; I will call it *natural femininity*. Not femininity the way women define it, nor the way men want us to be, or the way 1970s secular feminists have remade women to be like men. This natural femininity will not necessarily be the church's current definition of femininity either.

Natural femininity will be the things that God put in women to mirror himself. Time-bound characteristics are culturally created and re-created. Natural femininity is a permanent, timeless, essence that is in all women across cultures.

Natural femininity is not the same as what women "naturally" do or like. I thought wearing long skirts and having long hair was natural, but it certainly isn't when you're skiing or gardening, nor is it necessarily what God intended for women. Many women feel more feminine when they have acrylic nails and carry a purse with a small arsenal of makeup. What feels "natural" can have more to do with our culture or emotions at the moment. And with warped natures, it makes it even more important to cross-examine those things that feel natural.

Our compasses don't point north anymore. Our nature doesn't come naturally. And the world still groans over it.[37] That's what total depravity means, not that we're as bad as we'll ever be, but that there is crookedness in every soul capacity—our minds, desires, feelings, spirit, and will are all bent. We were made to run on God, but we'd rather do what feels "natural" and try to fill up on friends, on men, on babies, on jobs, on hobbies, on ourselves. Doing what comes naturally needs a refresh button. It needs the refreshment of the Spirit of God and his ideas in Scripture.

Redeeming Our Image

During my last year at UVA, I got engaged to a man I had dated for three years. In Marianne Dashwood exuberance, I planned nearly every wedding detail that summer: wedding dress, bridesmaids, groomsmen, church, tuxedos, and premarital counseling. Five months later, we broke off our engagement. In the grief and recovery from such a humiliating, unexpected experience, I met the man who would be my husband.

Dale and I dated for three months, and when he proposed I realized I wanted a new wedding dress. I just couldn't imagine putting on a dress that I had explicitly chosen for my ex-fiancé. Armed with practical reasons (the dress no longer fit because I had lost weight, and we had gotten a great deal on it), I asked my very practical father if he would spot me for another. He declined. I explained it all to Dale, apologizing again and again, telling him I wished I didn't have this "history," this baggage of a pre-planned wedding dress. It was not what I had hoped for. Dale listened and then folded me in his arms. After I was done crying, Dale took hold of my shoulders, stooped to look in my eyes, and announced, "Jonalyn, we're going to redeem that dress."

My mother and I rushed the gown to a tailor who managed to pin in and tuck away the bagginess. We added a few embellishments, a sheer bodysuit that gauzed my shoulders and arms to make it more appropriate for a winter wedding. When I put it on the morning of my wedding day, it fit like a glove. As I walked down the aisle on the arm of my father, I watched Dale's eyes. In his gaze, I felt no shame, no remorse. The dress had been bought back, it was redeemed.

The fall and judgment seared itself on women's bodies and souls; salvation and redemption is about remaking that scar. As deeply as the fall imprinted us, redemption can go deeper. Both men and women are fully qualified to receive redemption; we have what it takes: bruised and bleeding human souls. We are not what we should have been, but we can be remade. Like Dale remarked about my dress, God looks at us and says, "Woman, I'm going to redeem you."

Soul Care

1. What do you think Eve's soul was like before the fall? Try to describe her whole and healthy capacities: mind, will, feelings, spirit, and desire.
2. How do you think God's judgment changed Eve's body?
3. How do you think God's judgment changed Eve's soul? Be specific.
4. Do you need to discard any frivolous, flimsy, or flawed ideas of femininity?
5. What roles are you playing that are cramping your soul?
6. What areas of your soul are broken and need redemption? Think of each soul capacity: mind, will, feelings, spirit, and desire.
7. In preparation for the next chapter:

    Is weakness different from vulnerability? Can vulnerability be good? How?

a natural woman

If you strip off the flesh, are our souls essentially different?
Are we masculine and feminine on the soul level?

Ravi Zacharias

One evening in high school, I visited my grandmother's house for a splendid night of dining, reading, and classical music. While I was waiting for dinner to be ready, I walked up to a table that displayed her kaleidoscopes. She has had this collection since I was in grade school — it is a fixture at her home. The kaleidoscopes were artistically laid out, delicate cylinders of light sitting on a crisp, winter-white doily that was crocheted by her grandmother. I chose one as slender as a cigarette and held it up to the light. A symphony of color twisted in swirls and explosions, twirling and changing with my movements. This was a Picasso land, where light and movement directed form.

I exchanged the dainty silver one for a thick golden tube, sheathed in smoky emerald leather. Enticed by the feel of stamped craftsmanship in my hands, I held it up to my eye. There was a fat marble in the end of the peephole that lent its colors to the mirrors of the inner walls. I moved away from the window, noticing the way the darkness deepened the dance of color. Then I reached out and tried to jiggle the marble. It moved easily, you could twist it and change the patterned pictures. When Grandmother called me to get the drinks, I put the tube of color down on the table, walking away and thinking how another marble would change the experience entirely.

Natural femininity is your kaleidoscopic swirl of womanhood. Your soul provides the combination of color and light to the earth's need for woman. Your combination is like that marble; it is like no other and it changes and adds to the world's experience of woman. The mosaic of light and color in your soul is a gift that will be similar to other women and yet will be all uniquely yours: yours to discover, yours to enjoy, yours to give.

Cookie-Cutter Femininity

Since women are multifaceted and distinct, we cannot capture femininity in a list of five traits or three bullet points. It would reduce and stifle our womanhood, it would be like minimizing Vermeer's *Girl with a Pearl Earring* portrait to a paint-by-color drawing. I don't want to take a lovely picture of womanhood and scribble one code (like *emotional* or *helper*) all over it. I trust God to be more creative than that. Eugene Peterson writes, "God's creative genius is endless. He never, fatigued and unable to maintain the rigors of creativity, resorts to mass-producing copies. Each life is a fresh canvas on which he uses lines and colors, shades and lights, textures and proportions that he has never used before."[1]

Karl Barth, the twentieth-century theologian who wrote extensively about the sexes in his *Church Dogmatics*, thought such lists set up a "malicious caricature on the one side or the other, or perhaps both."[2] I want to avoid this type of caricaturing.

While an absolute list of essentials for every woman won't do, there are still some things that women share, feminine character traits that surface and resurface across centuries. Do we just call these things interesting, but point out all the exceptions to them? Or can we affirm them as, to quote Pope John Paul II, the "true genius of women"?[3] Can we find a way to list the similarities among women without making them absolute requirements? Or is femininity just too difficult to nail down?

How Philosophers Help Women

Femininity is not the only concept that is difficult to define. We have the same difficulty defining religion or art. Define religion as belief in God, and you leave out Buddhism. Call religion "any group of people who worship something," and you include too much, video gamers who worship their computers, some owners of pets, music groupies. Pornography is just as difficult. If you define porn as "pictures of naked people," you throw much of art out too. If you call it "pictures of naked people having sex," then you don't cover enough. Call it "pictures of sexy naked people," then you have to define "sexy." Some people say, "Any pictures of naked people are in poor taste, so get rid of them." Some people say, "I don't know how to define pornography, but I know it when I see it."

That last statement hints at another way. Philosophers define such slippery things using *family resemblance*, a list of the many ways things resemble each other. For instance, in my family I would list resemblances like curly hair, olive skin, brown eyes, thick hair, thin body frame, capacity for long-distance running and swimming, and so forth. Now, not everyone in my family has each of those characteristics. My dad has glowing white skin and blue eyes, and my Aunt Terri is not a long-distance runner. But here is the genius of family resemblances: you don't have to have all of them to be "in." *Family resemblances are a list of common but not required characteristics.* Philosophers use this approach to define art, pornography, religion, and even science. Making such lists allows us to see why certain things belong in a group, how each member fits this category without forcing every member into total conformity. We don't require that my dad wear brown contacts to "fit in." Or that my aunt train for half marathons. We know and accept that some members do not have all resemblances. They still are "in" the group because they have enough on the list. As a philosopher, I think this approach works well with femininity.

Family resemblance helps us explain femininity because it keeps our notions of femininity clear and yet flexible. We can come up with a list of recurring resemblances that many, though not all, women have. Some items on this list will be characteristics of many women, but all together they may not be true of every woman. The key is that all women will enjoy at least one of these family characteristics. One is sufficient for a woman to be feminine.

We have come to the threshold of womanhood, the core or essence of femininity, the thing that people talk about, dance around, struggle to define but seem to experientially know; we know a woman when we see one. Beth Moore, the speaker and Bible study leader, explained her intuition like this: "I don't think our bodies are the only things that make us male and female. They positively identify us as such, but I love thinking that we are also male and female in our immaterial essence. We will still be man and woman in heaven when we've been freed from these frail and temporary physical bodies."[4]

But what is this feminine essence? From literature to history to psychology to philosophy, we can cull a list of femininity's family resemblances, ways many women are, not the ways all women ought to be. You may identify with all of them or only one. A person has a woman's soul by having the first characteristic. The first family resemblance is something essential to all women. The rest are more commonalities that more women than men share, hence, *family resemblance.*

Freeing, Natural Femininity

Women are interwoven with a female body, so the first family resemblance is a soul that owns a female body. Beyond this, many women are vulnerable and interdependent. Many also have sensitive

	Family Resemblance	Description
1.	Female body	A soul interwoven into a female body
2.	Vulnerability	In body and soul
3.	Interdependence	Identity emerges from intimacy
4.	Sensitive awareness	Soul radar for others and ourselves
5.	Emotional intelligence	Experience in management of intense emotions
6.	Cultivation	Ability to tend others, ourselves, and the world

awareness and emotional intelligence, and many cultivate people and the world. These are just the beginning of a list of natural feminine resemblances — there may be more. These qualities, as gifts from God, may come more easily to us. These are not things we should have to try to do as much as they will be part of who we are. These characteristics are not limited to our romantic or church life; they will affect every area of our lives. Natural femininity is about how we use our souls. It is the dye in our souls, changing all of our capacities, orienting us to be women in the world.[5]

Soul Dye

You might already be comparing yourself to the feminine resemblances, measuring how many of these you have or don't have. For now, I must remind you (and myself) to stop. These are family resemblances; no one is "out" or less feminine for not having sensitivity or emotional intelligence. To say those with a higher number of resemblances are *more* feminine would be like saying my mother is more a part of my family because she has brown eyes. My father may look different because he doesn't have all the family resemblances, but that doesn't make him less a family member. In the same way, some women may not be sensitive or care about cultivating others, they may prefer to teach or pastor, and disdain children's work. This doesn't

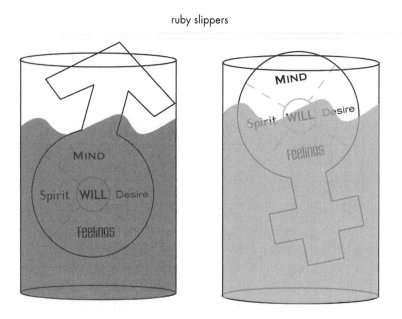

make them less feminine, it just makes them another natural variety of femininity.

Think of the resemblances of natural femininity like colors of dye. Any combination is a unique dye in your soul. You, however, must determine what swirl of color describes you. I cannot, your pastor cannot, your husband cannot. Each woman has the right and the responsibility to understand her own soul in perfect Christian freedom. No one should force a characteristic on you. This is not another corset to squeeze into, not another golden slipper to cram on. This is a wide drafting table to ask God to help you draw the depths and heights of your femininity. It is discovery time. Take a look at the potential of your ruby slippers.

It may sound like a lot of work. Why make the effort? I hope the resemblances of natural femininity will help women see how we are not alone. Like when I took the personality tests to learn I was more extroverted than introverted—I found out that there was a whole group of extroverts out there who understood how much I was recharged after meeting new people and how I loved interacting with groups of total strangers. Perhaps the discovery of your feminine resemblances will give you much the same experience. I hope the resemblances of natural femininity open up a place for you to meet other women as equals.

I have had the same hair stylist for years. She's watched me go from hiding my hair to highlighting and layering it to cutting bangs. She opened her shop early to curl my hair into ringlets for my wedding day. She knows my hair well. Besides curly hair, we don't have much in common, not God, family, home country, free time, hobbies, ideas about truth and goodness. We barely share the English language. In the scores of hours I've spent watching her alternately thin, cut, straighten, highlight, blow-dry, oil, and mousse, I can only think of one time I've seen her soul. It happened recently when we got to talking about having women's bodies. She just lit up with anger as she talked about how men stare. I looked through my folds of aluminum highlights and said, "Oh, you're like that too! I'm so glad I'm not alone." I talked about how I feel objectified and afraid when I jog. And in our womanhood we began to relate to one another.

Our womanhood might unite us. We might notice that we all have ruby slippers on, and yet these slippers are different, uniquely built for our feet to walk along God's highway. Our natural femininity might make us wonder if more women are like us, giving us a common ground to relax in our resemblances, rather than trying to force all women to be one brand of female, or the other extreme, denying that women are unique.

Kaleidoscope Femininity

Natural femininity is the way we live with our female body *and* the way we use our soul for vulnerability, interdependence, sensitive awareness, emotional intelligence, and cultivation. The latter five characteristics are not requirements for all women. A man may be sensitive, vulnerable, or a cultivator, but that doesn't make him feminine. A man can never be feminine in his soul because he doesn't have the essential ingredient: a female body.[6]

Last fall Dale and I spoke on gender and souls to a graduate class of psychologists. After I explained interdependence, one male laughed and said it described him perfectly. The fact that he shared a characteristic with many women did not mean this man was feminine. Instead it shows how his male soul shared a characteristic that more women own than men. I told him he was a gift to his female friends. He could relate to them in this area. He could be an interpreter and an advocate for them. But his interdependence was owned by a man's soul.

I have a problem in saying any man is feminine or any woman is masculine. When we encounter a woman who is matter-of-fact and straightforward (or a man who is sensitive and interdependent) perhaps we should get to know their version of femininity and masculinity before assuming they are "out of touch" with their gender. One more helpful hint: it is usually false to say that one woman is more feminine than another. She may just have more from the list of family resemblances. But as I said above, just because my mother may have more of the general qualities of a family member, doesn't make her more of a family member than my father.

I want to explain the specific uniqueness of each of the characteristics that constitute natural femininity, so you can take inventory of which are natural to you.

Resemblance #1: Inhabiting a Female Body

Our bodies change the way our souls work. Our very experience of life is female. This difference goes beyond baby-birthing, nursing, and menopause. When I was a sophomore in college studying abroad, I went to Paris for a haircut. For several years I had tried to get a short and sassy bob, but I kept getting cold feet and would end up with nothing more than a trim. But in France, even though the hair stylist stumbled through his English to get me to change my mind, I held my ground. I wanted it all cut off, *merci beaucoup*!

He shrugged, picked up a pair of shiny scissors, and pulled my hair back into a high ponytail. Then clip, clip, cut. I closed my eyes. When I opened them, he was dangling a ten-inch ponytail above my head. It looked like a dead, curly-haired animal. He began shearing off all but a one-and-a-half-inch circumference, a closely cropped halo of curls, which he lavishly gelled before whipping off my smock. I gazed at my reflection, mostly pleased.

I walked out feeling lighter, thinner, newer. I had cut my hair in Paris. It was a risk. I knew a certain male back home, someone I had been trying to impress, would hate it. "Women ought to have long hair," he had once said. My dad wouldn't like it either: "A woman's hair is her glory." I had grown up learning that lesson.

Yet the thing that propelled me into the salon and gave me the courage to shear off my "glory" was the way my hair had always plagued me. I wanted to remove the one thing that people always noticed, for good or evil. Anne of Green Gables would have understood. "God made my hair red on purpose, and I've never cared for him since."

Women have dieted, tanned, styled, dyed, and even cut their bodies in order to get that one marketed look. Few women have observed and lived with their bodies intentionally enough to enjoy owning them, as they are right now, not next month when I might be able to squeeze into my skinny jeans or after I have a baby when my breasts might swell a bit bigger. Not ten years ago when my stomach was a prepubescent flat washboard, but learning to be "in" my body and accept it right now. We don't want our bodies. This discontentment over our bodies is the first place we need Christ's help — to show us that women's bodies are a good thing.

My body is something I get to give over to my husband, a difficult task unless I actually believe that it is mine, part of me, and that my body is a good gift.[7] I know women who smirk and grimace when their husbands praise their bodies—confident that he is misguided, blind, or lying—or are embarrassed to have attention called to their flesh. They don't believe him or anyone else.

Until my body and soul are really my own possessions, I cannot present them to anyone. Writer Virginia Stem Owens asks a grippingly good question, "Can I be friends with myself if I am not friends with my body?"[8] To be friends with our bodies is a good form of self-possession, allowing us to own ourselves enough to be capable of giving ourselves away to God and others. What if we redefined our bodies with Christ as our first consultant, not fashion models, or our own hurtful standards? What if I asked Christ what he thinks of thick thighs, thin calves, flabby arms, and love handles? He may be more concerned at our attitudes toward our bodies than our bodies themselves. My body is something I get to steward, to love, to cherish, to be "in," to give, until death do us part. After death, I get a new one and I'm not certain it will look all that drastically different from this one. Job says, "Yet from my flesh I shall see God." It may be time to learn to like what I have been given.

We Are All Feminine

The one characteristic common to women is also the one thing we all struggle to own. If we cannot accept our bodies, how will we accept the other feminine characteristics? Because body care is part of the battleground for women, it could be the place where all women unite, the common ground where we might fight the lies, the advertising assaults, the Creed of Materialism, the temptations to be immodest. We could unite over what female embodiment means and how we ought to think of our femaleness. We could develop disciplines that are meant to help us stand strongly and vulnerably instead of attending to our looks, pitting her against us, comparing our body shapes, and running at each other with salty, dark eyes.

All women can commiserate over and laugh about our bodies' glory and mess. And when we're honest, we realize our experience is common; there is no hierarchy or isolation in some of these places. Every woman learns the experience of monthly cycles, either through menstruation, pregnancy, or lactation. Every woman knows the feeling of vulnerability when walking alone at night. Natalie, whose mother chased her with blush and powder around the house, took up boxing in her teens. Yet, Natalie knows the fear of walking alone at night the same as my friend Becca, who nearly had her black belt in karate. They know their physical vulnerability even though they have a larger, stronger skill set for defense. Every woman knows the experience of feeling objectified, of feeling a man's eyes bore into her figure. All women know how unwanted whistles, calls, hoots, and yells make us want to either strut our stuff or quickly walk away. We know how unsolicited suggestions or jokes make us feel. Most women have experienced the negative effects of having a weaker body, a lower status, and less respect and power, as well as seeing how their femaleness elicits certain responses. All women have lived knowing what it means to be responded to as "female."[9]

As German religious philosopher Hanna-Barbara Gerl-Falkovitz did research on the anthropology of the sexes, she found that "our body is the bearer and expression of something interior. In order to determine at least to some extent how women differ from men, the observation of the body serves as a principle of the female soul and mind."[10] When I travel alone, I get a full reminder of my womanhood. My body, its shape and curves and vulnerability, makes me view the world differently.

Resemblance #2: Vulnerable Vessels

"Husbands, live with your wives in an understanding way, showing honor to the woman as the weaker vessel."[11] Peter could have been slurring women, or he could have been explaining a difference. This verse has been coupled with one from Timothy to develop a case for women's nature being weak, by which is meant morally deficient, easily deceived, infantile, and scatterbrained.[12] I don't agree, not because I haven't met all these qualities in women, but because there are just as many deceived, weak, susceptible, and childish men. Where women are called childish, men are called impotent. Where women are called easily deceived, men are called easily seduced. Men and women are both stuffed with weakness. Peter is trying to show some difference between men and women, but we've landed on the wrong one.

There is a type of weakness that isn't impotent or childish or featherbrained. Paul talks about it in Romans when he says godly strength is perfected in weakness.[13] Paul says he is content with this type of weakness. For when he is weak, he found he and God were stronger.

God finds this weakness very good; he even identifies himself with it. The "weakness of God is stronger than men."[14] Jesus "was crucified because of weakness. For we also are weak in Him."[15] Theologian Dr. Sarah Sumner notes that "weakness" or *asthenēs* must mean something other than "inherent inferiority" since God cannot be inferior. She has translated the Greek word *asthenēs* into a more helpful word: "vulnerability, or a willingness to be responsive."[16] See how well it works: The *vulnerability* of God is stronger than men. Jesus was crucified because of *vulnerability*. Live with your wives ... as the more *vulnerable* vessel.[17] This word connects God with women. Bono, speaking more as philosopher than musician, said, "The one thing we can all agree, all faiths and all ideologies, is that God is with the vulnerable."[18]

Most women reject vulnerability. It is a difficult soul trait to eagerly embrace. We feel like our vulnerable bodies and souls make us more susceptible to attack. Maybe we're like Dorothy, the ruby slippers of our femininity are only a liability, pegging us as the main target for the Evil One.

We can reject our vulnerability, if we want. Peter isn't crystal clear that we are vulnerable vessels. It's a metaphor after all, "as the weaker vessel." That tiny word "as" means that if men treat their wives as if their wives were more vulnerable, their prayers will make it to God. If husbands treat their wives with tender love, they will see some of what God originally intended for man and woman, how we were intended to live side by side, taking dominion as joint heirs—once joint heirs of Eden, then of judgment, and now joint heirs of grace. Peter says treat her "as a fellow heir," and there's the "as" again. It's only fair to say that if women want the "as a fellow heir" to mean they are joint heirs, they ought to accept the "as the weaker vessel" to mean they are vulnerable, too. I think it is safe to assume both.[19]

We are physically vulnerable.[20] In some Christian circles, vulnerability of body "proves" that women are weak minded, weak spirited, and weak willed. Our vulnerability continues to be exaggerated and then exploited just as it was in the garden by the Evil One.

This exploitation doesn't have to be intentional; often it is not. My husband refused a pink marker once because it was a "sissy color." When I told him his words hurt my feelings, he didn't understand. I felt embarrassed to have voiced it, even "overly sensitive" to have felt like that. I spent a long time trying to figure out why. I think what bothered me is not that he doesn't like pink (that's no problem), but that he disliked the color on the basis of it being sissylike. The very word "sissy" can mock a woman's vulnerability. It turns her willingness to be open and transparent into a laughable, impotent weakness. Dale was amazed, but he agreed that it made sense.

I think we need to claim our physical vulnerability as the material we have now after the fall. This will not mean women are more fragile of mind or dwarfed in soul than men. "Vulnerable" expresses our difference better than "weak," since vulnerability can distinguish women physically from men without communicating any mental or moral deficiency. Like a good plot of earth that responds to a gardener's touch, our bodies are more vulnerable. This means we have more to enjoy and more to fear on earth. This doesn't mean women are incapable of handling the hard knocks of life, or that we become hysterical in the face of battle. God created Eve to be capable of fighting alongside Adam, an *ezer*, helping him when the Evil One attacked. She was sufficient to stand with him. In fact, Eve wouldn't have been much help to Adam if he had to shoulder more "final decision making" and her ultimate spirituality. I think when God made Woman as *ezer*, she was completely helpful, not hindering, to Man.

Woman: Made from Living Flesh

God was intentional about making Woman, committing an entire section of the creation account to her. God made Woman's body, not out of a clay mold, but out a piece of living flesh.[21] Woman's original material was more vulnerable than man's; she was made out of living cells.[22] Vulnerability requires that we have places that are tender, places we can be affected, touched, and even destroyed. A sparrow is more vulnerable than a rock. But because a sparrow is alive, it interacts, whistles, and soars, even though it can also be caught by a cat and clawed to death.

I often thought of Woman's beginnings as more evidence that Woman wasn't important enough for God to make first. Now I think God made Woman second because he needed the appropriate human, living material, to form her. Woman is the only creature who was created from a piece of *living* flesh. Perhaps this indicates something different about our souls.[23]

Woman began life unafraid of her vulnerability. Woman's body was made out of life, her first experience and environment was *with* another. She glided from life with God (he made her while man was asleep, bringing her to him) into a comradeship with Adam. She experienced human interaction soon after her creation. She exists and immediately is known. The first words Eve hears is the language of another loving her back. She awakens to be needed and loved. She lives and is quickly united to another.[24] There are no long hours of naming and waiting and feeling alone. There is no word of domination, or even loving dominion. No one took advantage of her vulnerability, until the Serpent arrived.

On one of our thousand-mile trips from Los Angeles to Colorado, my husband and I drove different cars. We caravanned along I-15 and then I-70 until, in the middle of the night, Dale exited in front of me. Perhaps it was because we had been driving for so many hours, perhaps it was because I was distracted and rather tired, but as he exited, I barreled past him. Dale called my cell phone to tell me I was out there by myself and could I please turn around. Unfortunately, the exits were few and far between in that section of Utah. I told him I would pull over and wait for him. He shouted down that idea because he did not want me sitting alone, an easy target in the middle of the highway, far from him, far from lighted areas, and far from civilization. He told me to drive slowly and he would try to catch up. Then we lost reception. Then my cell phone died.

I slowed down, driving 40 miles an hour on a road with a limit of 75. For a lonely hour, semi-trucks and spooky, dark vans whizzed by. Every time I saw a pair of headlights in my rearview mirror, I would tell myself that it was Dale, coming to join me. And every time, it was another unfamiliar vehicle. I felt horribly vulnerable, because I knew there were men who preyed on the weak, and here I was blocked off from any connection to husband or cell phone or help. I was not in a world that looks kindly on scared young women driving at three a.m. by themselves.

Since Genesis 3, the world has been peopled with men and women who act like the Serpent, preying on the vulnerable. In response, how many women do you think embrace their vulnerability?

Soul Care for Vulnerable Vessels

Think of an activity you prefer doing with a friend — be it swimming in the ocean or walking home late at night. When I wade into the large waters of the Pacific at Huntington Beach, I much prefer a companion. It is the same with exploring the woman's soul. We need to wade through our similar embodied experiences together. These experiences of body life could be opportunities to grow and struggle in community. We might find that caring for our vulnerability helps us enjoy being female.

Soul care is attention to the inside. It starts with noticing our beliefs and desires, choices and emotions. Before trying to change our behavior, what do we think about being vulnerable? How do you respond to the statement, "Women are more vulnerable and, therefore, weaker than men"? Does it make you sad, thankful, angry? It's no surprise that the root of vulnerable means "to wound." It sounds unpleasant; no wonder we don't want to think about it. But soul care means we must, it means that we sit in the vulnerability puddle and splash around. We might even look for ways to find vulnerability a necessary and good thing.

There is a physical and symbolic act where a man and woman write their love with their bodies. They imprint on their flesh their attraction and amazement in the other. Men who love women are like women who love men; they are in search of the deeper places, not just a phallus-vagina meeting, but the hidden places in her soul. Men have attested to it again and again. It is not the act that is wanted, but the person. As Mike Mason, a one-time monk who decided to marry, explains in his meditation on marriage, God "made the woman with an open wound in her body, such that it can only be stanched by a man; and the man he made with a tumor, the maddening pressure of which is only alleviated when it is allowed to grow inside the woman's wound. He made the man to root and to flower in the aching earth of a woman."[25]

Sex is both a uniting and pro-creating recreation. It turns the most vulnerable parts of us into the tools for recreation, delight, pleasure, beginnings. It is a picture of what we want to do with our souls—unite, yes of course, but also of the way a woman opens herself to a man, proving that her physical vulnerability is also strength. Dr. Jerry Root, a Wheaton professor and friend who married Dale and me, shared how he saw his wife's tears as an emotional act of vulnerability, no less sexy than her breasts and no less alluring than her invitation to bed.

In listening to the voice of your culture, perhaps you've imagined that there is no need for sensitive, vulnerable women, or that openness is a surefire way to brokenness. Listen to what Paul says: "It is much truer that the members of the body which seem to be weaker (*asthenēs*, the same Greek word as in 1 Peter's 'the weaker vessel') are necessary; and those members of the body which we deem less honorable, on these we bestow more abundant honor, and our less presentable members become much more presentable."[26] It is not only feminine, but human to be vulnerable, receptive, and tender. Perhaps women have a head start. Perhaps women's physical vulnerability can become a starting ground for soul vulnerability.

One of the key traits I want in friends is soul vulnerability. It's one of the things we love about Jesus. When he shares his fear in Gethsemane, when he cries over Lazarus, when he screams on the cross, we shudder, and we love him. We know whereof he speaks. We have a place where we relate to God, and we know that God has come near.

When a woman shares her frustrations over her sex life, or her inadequacies in child rearing, or the frightening gap between her life and her life goals, she is both weak and strong. She is strong because she is honest about her weakness. She has strength because truth is strongly manifest in her. And when she is both vulnerable and strong, she is a picture of God on earth.

In the film *The Terminal*, Catherine Zeta-Jones plays an unstable, sexy stewardess. We first see her wearing terribly high stilettos, which make it easy for her to slip big-time on a huge, unmarked wet floor.

Her bag goes flying and her right heel pops off. Cursing and flustered, she quickly snatches the slender point of plastic and stuffs it into her purse. Gathering her bag, she hops up and keeps walking. As we watch her stride away, we can't tell that she's missing one pointed heel, not unless we look closely at the base. There is a four-inch space where the heel ought to be. She walks with the height, the grace, and the self-confidence of a woman in well-fitting heels, but she is faking it. She won't let you notice her weakness.

I don't want to be like the Catherine Zeta-Jones character. Yet when I laugh at her, I'm also laughing at myself. Often I have spent time and money suppressing and covering up my weaknesses, fearful of my vulnerability, fearful of identifying too closely with my Lord. But when a woman is vulnerable, she glorifies God in sharing her weaknesses.[27] She marries honesty and transparency in her soul, and in doing so, images God.

Vulnerable women are Godlike. For the best picture we have of God is that of a man wrapped in a cloth washing feet.[28] He could lower himself, exposing his white belly, because he knew that the Father had given him all things and that he came from God and was going back to God.[29] He didn't have to grab power, because he knew someone had already given him all. His hands were vulnerable, open to feel the muck from toe-jammy feet — his hands were open because he had been given everything. This is why he could wash the dust off his betrayer, the man who would walk with those well-scrubbed feet to deliver him to death. Because of Jesus's belief in who God was and who he was, he could lower himself. Jesus, the human being, emptied of glory, with arms strained against rough-hewn wood, dying, while all of heaven watched the extent of his humility, shows us what it means to be human and vulnerable.

This is why we can embrace soul vulnerability, even when it feels like we are lessened by the confession. If we build up the belief in our own minds that we have a God watching our back, guarding our souls, keeping every treasure intact for us, we might risk more.[30] I desire this, to have this kind of vulnerability when I speak or teach or pray. My emotions don't embrace it though. I feel uncomfortable and afraid. But I still desire it.

I can build my desire. I can surround myself with friends who are not surprised when I fail, who don't look shocked or disapproving when I lose my temper, who thank me for being a fellow ragamuffin on the journey, friends who thank me for being honest when I explain how overwhelmed I feel, how I hate this job or these dogs, how I can't get everything done, how I'm behind and can't keep up. Friends who say something like what my dad said to a longtime friend who confessed he had lied to bolster his achievements. "That's okay," my dad replied, "I didn't love you for how great you thought you were."

I need that safe place. To know that nothing I do can make you love me any less or any more. I need to know that when I bleed, other people will watch with the tenderness to blot the blood without rebuke, without suggestion, and without surprise.

Resemblance #3: Interdependence

Between dependence and independence lies the overlooked land of interdependence.[31] Interdependence is more than depending on each other to get a task done, like the spokes of the wheel depend on the hub. We're all interdependent in this way. The interdependence that colors our souls is when *our identity emerges from within our intimacy*, when we see ourselves as "me in relationship" rather than "me as autonomous."[32]

Because I am interdependent, my beliefs are formed out of what others think about me. I desire to be needed by others. Relationships provide the means for me to understand my past, my goals, my character, my work, and my methods; and I emotionally want that. My thoughts regularly revolve around what they said or what she suggested, or what he noticed. I choose to have long conversations and drawn-out discussions to make sure everyone is content and understands me, and I, them. My will may need the buttressing of others' encouragement.

Sometimes interdependence comes in an unhealthy form of people pleasing. But I cannot really stop caring about others' opinions. I might be able to pretend I don't care, but it would be more to please someone than because I really don't care. The best way for an interdependent person to grow out of excessive people pleasing is to be more interdependent with the Godhead—to live before the audience in heaven. This requires that we know God, what he thinks, and how he feels about who we are becoming.

Interdependence is not a difference in quantity or intensity of relationships. Both men and women have full-blooded, healthy relationships. Men may enjoy interdependence as well, just not usually as predominantly or consistently as women; fewer men want this identity-intimacy connection.

Two Ways of Knowing

Interdependent women often rely on connected knowing, where you believe someone in order to connect with them. Independent women often rely on separate knowing, where you doubt someone in order to mine out the truth.

Connected knowers wait and listen, not because we don't know what to say or we have no opinion on the subject, but because we trust others to reveal the information first. Connected knowers may appear unthoughtful or even slow and gullible when we are actually using our minds and wills for forbearance. We are trying to be attentive and patient to new ideas, all the while holding back the itch for closure. Depending on how successfully or easily you hold back the itch may indicate your natural tendency for connected knowing.[33] Of course, anyone could learn this skill to some degree, but many women come by it naturally.

Connected knowing requires peer relationships, where we sit across from one another — not above, not below — and enter into each other's experiences. Connected knowers look at our friends' experience as something we can try to enter into. For connected knowers, no human experience is too foreign. We want to slip on other people's shoes and imagine what their life is like.[34] For instance, I may not have experienced sexual infidelity, but when a friend tells me about her husband's affair, I will piece together the smaller experiences of unfaithfulness in my life in order to enter her world. I listen and enter into that world with her, connecting in order to know and understand. That way I can say to her, "I see what you mean."

Connected knowing is most commonly used in stories. You must believe and enter that make-believe world if you want the magic to work. You must read the first lines of *The Wonderful Wizard of Oz* believing in the gray landscape, the gray house, and gray Aunt Em. You have to trust that when Frank L. Baum says the only spot of color in the whole state of Kansas was the pink bloom in Dorothy's cheeks, he knows what he's talking about. If you don't believe this, the story will never weave its spell. Maybe that's why more women enroll in literary programs. As one psychologist put it, "Many women find it easier to believe than to doubt."[35]

Separate knowers question, doubt, and try to find the contradiction in new information. It's usually linked with a posture of independence, separate and often unengaged, in order to get at the truth of the matter. New information is a chance to practice combat, like a bouncer at an exclusive club. Separate knowers are more eager to rebuff and send away ideas without proper identification. I experienced a lot of separate knowing in seminary; most academic settings (particularly male-dominated fields) favor this mode of knowing. Separate knowers are often skeptical throughout the argument, and when they eventually do agree, there is not an understanding, let-me-enter-into-your-world moment. They just agree and add the new idea to their belief structure.

While separate knowers have claimed to own all the rational territory for centuries, both connected and separate knowledge can be rational. Both types of knowledge require evaluation, reasoning, induction, and deduction. They just choose different times and ways to display these skills. The difference in these two ways of knowing has enormous consequences, from how we make friends, to how we learn, to how we interact with God.

At this point, I ought to add that most people use both connected and separate knowing, though we usually prefer one over the other. We feel most comfortable with one. I can act like a separate knower and play the devil's advocate—I learned the skill at home as a young teen. My father and I would go back and forth in sparring matches during dinnertime, questioning, doubting, cross-examining each other. It was exciting for me, but I know that even when I won the match, I felt separated from my dad. The knowledge was sweet, but I didn't like feeling separated. Separate knowing didn't build my emotional connection with my father. Though debating with him was exciting on one level, what I really wanted was to know and understand him. I didn't want to prove or disprove an abstract argument. I couldn't relax in the debate because I was all the while wondering if he or I was going to get our feelings hurt. To me it wasn't all fun and games. It wasn't really between our positions, it was between persons. So while I can perform as a separate knower, I prefer connected knowing.[36] It comes more naturally to me.

Connected knowers enjoy learning that is connected, which is usually personal and particular, grounded in firsthand experience. Edith Stein, one of the pioneers of women's soul work, wrote that woman is "directed to the concrete, the individual, and the personal; she has the ability to grasp the concrete in its individuality and to adapt herself to it, and she has the longing to help this peculiarity to its development."[37]

Connected knowers prefer learning from others' experience. Tell us the story and we cannot doubt, belittle, or marginalize it, at least not justly. I just eat up the experience of others. I don't want to know the rule book on being a good daughter or getting married, as much as I want to know how you transitioned into adulthood or what worked in your wedding. It's the personal stuff that I trust, that I remember enough to write in my journal or repeat to my friends.

Women's conversations are often practical. Eve's conversation with the Serpent indicates that the craftiest of all beings knew that this woman cared about practical stuff. He doesn't command or challenge her like he did with Jesus. "If you are the Daughter of God then prove it and eat this fruit." He doesn't say, "If you're the image of God and in charge of the earth, why don't you take dominion over this tree too?"

He gets personal. "Your eyes, Eve, will be opened."

He gets practical. "And you will be like God."

He is crafty, and she is deceived. He lures her with a practical how-to-improve list, and she bites. This first woman's temptation was customized for her, tailored to wiggle in and weaken her soul's strengths. And she was deceived.

Connected knowing gives women the advantage of regularly practicing equality and empathy. Look at interdependent women when they hear a testimony of grief. Women often enter the speaker's pain as they listen. One psychological study found that giving more emotional feedback through facial expressions will actually predispose you to feel more, expect more.[38] Our smiling or frowning faces intensify our emotions. Since women are often more facially expressive, it makes sense that we actually do feel more empathetic, engaged, and connected.[39] Our facial feedback predisposes us toward interdependence.

Connected knowing can hurt us too. Connected knowing might make us desire to please others more than we desire truth. Or we might rely on another opinion before trusting our own spirit. The latter was Eve's problem.

Interdependent women grow in strength as they grow in relationship. From wedding showers, slumber parties, makeover parties, ladies' book clubs, female discussion groups, scrapbook marathons, women's gyms, and women's Bible studies, our conversation is often heavy with empathizing and connecting words. As an interdependent woman, I am learning to accept that this is who I am, someone who is forging her identity from the relationships with others. This is the soul I have been given to cultivate and offer to God so that he might grow me. But it is not the only way to be feminine.

Resemblance #4: Sensitive Awareness

When we first started dating, Dale introduced me to G. K. Chesterton. I quickly fell in love with the writings, the paradoxical turns of phrase of this British journalist and Christian apologist. Chesterton gave me permission to believe that the fairy tales are worth revisiting if we mine out the truths embedded in them. As he wrote in his enchanting defense of "The Ethics of Elfland," "My first and last philosophy, that which I believe in with unbroken certainty, I learnt in the nursery ... The things I believed most then, the things I believe most now, are the things called fairy tales. They seem to me to be the entirely reasonable things."[40]

They can be time-tested beacons pointing to good desires and hopes we treasured as young girls. They can also be too idealistic and harmful as we build up an arsenal of expectations that no man and no God could ever fulfill.

Women who are interdependent may struggle to accept that they are sensitively aware, because it is easy to ignore our sensitivity in order to avoid the "high-maintenance" stigma. We may care so deeply about other people's opinions that we don't even know our own thoughts. If you have both interdependence and sensitive awareness, it will be even more important to pay attention to what you loved in your childhood. These folk and fairy stories have helped me see who I was before I downplayed and distanced myself from my gift for sensitivity.

As a young girl, one of my favorite stories was about the prince who wanted to marry a real princess. Though many women approached him, claiming they were of royal blood, he was never quite sure they were real princesses.

One night, when the rain was running in torrents down the castle walls, a maiden knocked at the door. Rain flowed down her legs, into her shoes, dribbling out at the toes. Despite her torn and bedraggled appearance, she claimed to be a real princess.

Inviting the princess in, the queen secretly set out to prove her wrong. The queen commanded her servants to place a tiny pea under twenty thick mattresses and twenty eiderdown quilts. They towered several stories high in one of the castle's largest rooms. The princess had to climb a tall ladder to get into bed.

When the princess went to bed, she couldn't sleep a wink. She woke up unhappy, grumpy, and bruised. When the queen asked her how she had rested, she complained:

"Oh, wretchedly! Heaven knows what might have been in the bed, but I lay upon something hard, so that my whole body is black and blue. It was really dreadful."[41] The queen, surprised, but quite pleased, announced that only a princess could have felt the hidden pea through twenty mattresses and twenty eiderdown quilts.

"You are truly a real princess," she said and presented her to the delighted prince.

I loved it. The story was called *The Real Princess*, a title I like much better than *The Princess and the Pea*. When I take the time to return to this beloved childhood story, I am reminded that under my to-do list and goals for the month lies a desire for a story like *The Real Princess*.

The princess is aware and sensitive, but she is not scolded for it. Amazing and glorious, the servants don't tell her to stop being so fussy. The queen isn't shocked, and she doesn't dismiss this "high-maintenance" girl out of her palace and away from her son. The princess is not catechized to "give thanks in all circumstances." All the court, the knights, the nobles, the queen, and the prince praise her. Because of her sensitivity, she is deemed an equal for the prince.

Because of her sensitivity she is real. She is honored for something we usually try to stamp out of ourselves. She is appreciated and rewarded for her sensitivity. *The Real Princess* affirms something that is slowly rubbed off, cut away, or anesthetized in women's souls.

Woman's Soul Radar

Call it womanly intuition or Mom having eyes in the back of her head. Or if you're neuropsychiatrist Louann Brizendine, you'd call it "having giant, invisible antennae that reach out into the world, constantly aware of the emotions and needs of those around you."[42] It's probably best described as our soul's ability to know other people's souls. Sensitive awareness, like a radar detector, sweeps wide and quickly across a room. I can walk into a room and instantly get a "read" on the situation. I'll see my husband in front of his desk and know—by his posture, his eyes, the speed of his typing, the slope of his shoulders, and the way he interacts or disregards me—what he is *feeling*. It doesn't mean I'm always correct, but I'm always getting signals.

Sensitive women will know how to read the message between the lines. Perhaps they are like the young girls in one study who, as early as twelve months, responded to distress in others through something as simple as a comforting, sympathetic look or vocal inflection. Girls have a better awareness of what might be a social faux pas before boys learn to understand such social rules.[43] When they grow up, many women are better at reading the emotions on a person's face.

A sensitive woman might say, "I know she said she was excited to see me, but I'm sure she didn't mean it." It makes sense, too, that Dr. Janet Hyde found in her meta-analysis that women outscore men in indirect aggression.[44] Both men and women are aggressive, just more women (not all) will communicate their anger indirectly. We pick up criticism—sometimes imagined, sometimes real—about our clothes, body, makeup, lifestyle, ideas, occupation, and kids. And we know how to dish it out too. The criticism might be intended. It might not. When we feel criticized or hurt, it doesn't help to hear people say, "Stop being so sensitive." You might as well tell me to turn off my soul, to deaden part of my natural femininity, shutting off a part of the way I see, feel, know, and choose. I cannot stop sensing these things. I cannot turn the radar off. I can ignore it or stuff it. Or I can use it as material to grow through. Just because I'm naturally sensitive does not give me a right to act out on my radar detection. I might be wrong about it, after all. I might need to both acknowledge and control the thought.

Marketers use women's radar detection to get us to notice more and buy more. If we act out on all our sensitive awareness without self-control, we would probably buy even more scented bath products, home fragrances, perfume, creamy sheets, silky camisoles, cuddly toys for our dogs to shred, warm afghans, and fuzzy pajamas. With wider radar, we notice the detail and variations. Finely painted china, immaculate gardens, and spotless homes all draw our eyes. We can wonder together what to do with our observations. Do we compare, do we marvel, do we admire, do we envy, do we buy, or do we just enjoy?

Author Gary Chapman made a big splash with the release of his book *The Five Love Languages*. I'm not certain all people have one dominant love language, or that there are only five, but I think he was right that we give love in the way we want to receive it. If I love receiving flowers, chocolates, and back rubs, it is because I have sensitivity to the time and thought put behind those things. I notice the details. My sensitivity radar is attuned to them, even if I don't say so, even if I don't demand it, even if I never admit it. Many men do not notice. This isn't to say they're insensitive, just that they are not tuned in to the radar. In one scene from the beloved Angela Thirkell novels, David, an incorrigible, self-interested flirt, sits between two jealous females. "Mutual hatred passed between the girls in waves. Hatred for David also permeated the air, but to none of these currents did David appear to be attuned."[45]

The sensitivity of many women may explain the perpetual disagreement between men and women about humor. In general, men find it funny when someone else is the butt of a joke. To cut a friend down, insult, or berate him is funny and is usually just ribbing in good fun. Women, however, tend to target themselves; it is more humorous to joke about one's own failed knitting project than to mock a friend's knitting disaster. In fact, I cannot even conceive of a group of women laughing at a failed tea party or a failed essay paper, and the hostess or author finding the joke in it. Perhaps this difference is behind the hurt wife's protest, "Don't say that. It's mean!" And the husband's baffled reply, "I was only joking." I regularly hear men point out their guy friends' errors or botch ups, hunting for the inadequacies to laugh about. Women's humor, in contrast, is usually self-deprecating. Perhaps it is because women seem to know how to poke fun at themselves without risking offense. Men may quite easily poke too hard at a friend, but most men don't pick up any subtle passive aggression.

Sometimes I feel I must tell Dale to stop ribbing because he's making someone upset. He will stop when it's a woman because he knows I have the radar to pick up her discomfort. If it's a guy, Dale will turn right back to me and say with a smile, "Relax, it's the way guys talk."

Redeeming Sensitivity

What do you think of when you hear the word "sensitive"? Do you think of a decorative porcelain figurine, a crystal vase, or a high-powered telescope? Sensitivity describes more than just touchy, twitchy women. Sensitivity is about fine quality and precise function; a microscope is sensitive, as is a beating heart. To tell a woman to toughen up, or to "stop being so sensitive" is like clipping the wings of a bird. You never get to see the full plumage in her wingspan or watch her soar and plummet in freedom. A woman's sensitivity can be a mark of vulnerable strength.

Some women show their sensitivity best when they act as hostess, others when they counsel, others when they listen. My mom can do the first so well. When she hosts a party at her home, her sensitive side gets a chance to shine. It's like putting a diamond ring under the lights at a jewelry store. All of a sudden you see rainbows, sparkles, and a brilliant explosion of light. Her mind darts to all the things her guests might need: dessert, a cold drink, sleep, towels, more hot water, less breeze from the window, sugar, cream, sugar substitute, lactose pills, popcorn, napkins, lemonade, less noise, softer music, no dog, more dogs, less cats. And she manages to meet all these needs while smiling. She loves to do it.[46]

To someone who isn't naturally sensitive, this might seem nearly neurotic. And it could be, I suppose, except we seek it out, we thrive in it. We actually love sensing all the needs around us. When the people at my home are having a good time, when I get to bask in the glow of talking, eating, sharing, and living, I see the body of Christ triumphant and freed. I feel an enormous sense of value and accomplishment. My soul glows and pulses with the life in my home.

This is partially why many women excel in hospitality. We are sensitive to needs where a man may see none, or only a few. Because we see, we respond. The apostle Paul knew women could do that. He praises women (in this case, widows) who have turned their sensitive awareness to the needs of others around them. He admires them for doing good things for others, bringing up children, showing hospitality to strangers, washing fellow believers' feet, assisting those in distress.[47] His entreaty for young widows to get married and "keep house" is not to imprison women in the kitchen or in the nursery.[48] Paul wanted to encourage women to discipline their bodies to one place in order to free their souls from the prison of gossip, sensuality, idleness, and greed.[49]

One of my favorite gardening days was when my friend Lisa joined me for five hours of rosebush trimming. She and I unsheathed our clippers and attacked the unsuspecting Iceberg roses' mildewed leaves. We piled the clippings high in the trash can. When they got too high, we took turns clambering up and leaping onto the mounded piles of thorns, treading them down. I remember watching Lisa propelling the large trash cans around the yard without any problem. She and I love using our strength. We worked out in high school to *Arms & Abs of Steel* videos. We'd write notes to each other with Proverbs 31:17 in the signature, "She girds herself with strength and makes her arms strong." Lisa is also sensitive; she knows how to notice the double meaning in my tone. Her questions and awareness are traits I value in her. Her sensitivity and strength work in her feminine soul effortlessly, like a waltz. She reminds me that sensitive women, like God, are not weak.

It wasn't until I was in graduate school that I began to realize that there were certain good things about being sensitive. In college, I'd viewed sensitivity as a weakness, a deficiency; it was even an insult. But in my midtwenties, I began to appreciate that I could read the subtle messages between the lines.[50] I could read the nonverbal language people gave me, glimmering nuances in remarks, tone, and body language. I always had a steady stream of awareness of other people, not simply about the content of their experiences, but of the experience in their content. It wasn't always accurate, but I was always picking up where other people were sensitive.

Psychologists will often point out that such sensitivity has been socialized into women. It's a result of women being shoved down by patriarchy, they say. Some psychologists think women's sensitivity is only a matter of social pressure, upbringing, and gender roles. Dr. Sara E. Snodgrass's study on interpersonal sensitivity found that sensitivity is not as much gender specific as much as it's role specific. Whether man or woman, the subordinate is more sensitive to the leader, than the leader to the subordinate. Snodgrass tested men and women in both positions and noted that it was the position that produced the sensitivity, not the gender. Women showed no more signs of being sensitive when they were leading than men did.[51] Therefore, since most women are in subordinate positions, she surmised, whether at work or at home, women have learned to be more sensitive.

That explains the difference sociologically, but it discounts the physical difference between men and women. If women are physically more vulnerable, then they are constantly subordinate to men's strength. Most women could, if men wished, be shoved down. It is because of gentlemen that women can complain and push and nag; if brute force were used, few scrawny men and even fewer women would rise to any leadership. Though Snodgrass may be correct that a subordinate role produces sensitivity, women's physical vulnerability forces us into subordination whenever a man fails to be a gentleman. We are physically weaker in upper body, and this, perhaps more than any other repercussion from the judgment in Eden, has kept women subservient. This alone may have grown sensitivity in our souls, out of sheer social survival, whether we like that or not.

Think back to Hyde's cumulative gender study, a summary of past gender report summaries, covering hundreds of thousands of men and women. Some women are more sensitive, indicated by more women who have a tendency toward smiling, observing other's emotions, tendermindedness, and dislike for casual sex.[52] These differences, though not universal, far outstripped the differences in stereotypical areas like girls' talkativeness or boys' aggression and mathematical aptitude. One of my favorite series of studies in Hyde's summary was on baby girls' facial expression processing. Girls' ability to recognize and respond to faces ranged from a small to a large difference depending on the study. In all the studies, however, more baby girls identified faces than baby boys.[53]

The day I was born, the nurses laid me in a bassinet so my exhausted mother could recover. When my grandpa came to visit, he walked over to smile at me. His first words were in Spanish, "*Que esta haciendo alli?*" (What are you doing there?) He's told me the story so many times that I know exactly what I did. I smiled. He tells me, "You were ready to jump out with that smile." Then he'll look at whoever else might be listening to his story, "And only one day old!"

I think I am naturally sensitive — it is a gift wrapped into my femininity, a part of my ruby slippers, a color of natural femininity in my kaleidoscope. It is something I can use for good or evil. I can use my sensitivity as a radar detector, picking up subtle signals so I can be careful of others, so I can be intentional and caring about gift giving, letter writing, phone calling, meal making. Or I can use sensitivity like a lint brush, picking up dirt and crud on people, creating unwarranted suspicion and false expectations. Indeed, women who are gifted with sensitivity have a challenge — to use this gift not to cut people down, but to build people up.

Resemblance #5: Emotional Intelligence

Emotional intelligence is when we understand and direct our emotions with healthy control, so that our emotions play dedicated servant roles in our lives. Emotional intelligence involves knowing our emotions, using them to motivate ourselves, and being able to recognize emotions in others. It's also known as "heart knowledge" or interpersonal skills.[54]

If we are emotionally intelligent, we know our emotions enough to label them, sort them, and order them. I realize it sounds like a skill and in some ways it is, but women have more opportunity to work on the skill. Every day many women experience more emotions than many men. Two women to every one man have a wider emotional vocabulary.[55] In a study comparing daily emotional patterns between men and women, husbands and wives kept a log of their conversations. Overall, the women had a more positive attitude toward disclosing their vulnerable, hostile, or regretful emotions than did their husbands.[56] None of this, of course, means that men do not feel emotions. However, since women display more emotions, have more extensive emotional vocabularies, and tend to feel more open toward feeling lots of emotions, perhaps we have a fuller emotional life.

We may not feel validated or impressed with our emotions, but we know them very well. Because of our spectrum of emotional experience, we may be the most skeptical of a concept like emotional intelligence. We might even consider the idea an oxymoron.

In graduate school I found Daniel Goleman's book *Emotional Intelligence*. The title alone seemed to give my emotional capacity a chance to be transformed into a full-fledged part of my humanity.[57] Goleman notices how people with high IQs can be "stunningly poor pilots of their private lives."[58] Like the young college student who observed a small fire in his dorm. He got up to retrieve the fire extinguisher, returned to his room, and put out the flames. Nothing was unusual except the young man walked both ways. He felt no urgency, fear, or panic. He was a man of little emotional intensity; he was passionless. On the other end of the spectrum is a woman who lost her favorite pen and was distracted and discouraged for several days.[59] For Goleman, emotional intelligence indicates more about success and personal satisfaction than even IQ.

Emotional Servants

Emotional intelligence is something God endows to many women, like an endowment for the arts. It's something more natural to us, not because we are weak or needy or cursed, but because our bodies take in more emotional data. We have more emotions coming into our souls. We receive a lot of emotional input because we have a body that picks up more. When I move in the world, my body picks up more sensation just because my body is more vulnerable.

If we lift a heavy load of bricks, it creates more strain on our arms. Drilling holes in the wall creates more stress on my biceps than it does on my husband's. For me, it's easy to get annoyed when my body is strained. Emotions like annoyance and grumpiness ride piggyback on sensations like burning muscles. Our bodies receive automatic painful experiences: from cramps once a month, to delivering babies, to nursing, to menopause. These are the obvious ones.[60] The feeling of pain is often accompanied or followed with an emotion: irritation, annoyance, fear, anxiety, impatience, anger, joy, serenity. We experience more positive sensations too. Women's orgasms last longer than men's. Women's joy is different in birth, nursing, and weaning a child.

Since women have more sensations, we also have more emotions to know, sort, and order. If we saved up even a fraction of the time we pour into our appearance, our wardrobe, our hobbies, our television watching, we could find the time to organize our emotions. The propensity for more emotions isn't so much a liability as a chance to learn about our feelings. How do you feel about your emotions? What is your reaction to your own tears? Do you store them up as milestones in your growth, saving the moment, like God does, in a bottle to remember?[61] Or do we really hate crying, especially in front of others, because, well, it's embarrassing, it's messy, it's inconvenient, it's unprofessional. Women tend to experience and know their emotions sooner and faster. By the time we're in high school we've developed a sophisticated management system for processing, labeling, and filing our emotions. Our filing system might be healthy or it might be a system of stuffing, blame, or denial.

Our female bodies provide different material for our souls to work with. Women respond to the loss of youthfulness and aging very differently than men. What are your emotional responses over a bad hair day, the wrong hair dye, or a bad haircut? How do you respond to comments made about your body? Most women work with more creams, more makeup, more hair products, more skin-care products, and more hair removal than men. What effect does all this time, energy, and attention have on our soul's emotions?

Dallas Willard wrote that emotions make "wonderful servants, but terrible masters."[62] If we have more emotions flooding our soul's gates, then, ironically and blessedly, we also have more servants. It's time to put them to work.

Putting the Servants to Work

Imagine a shiny yellow tray on a work desk. This tray is your soul's emotional inbox. As you feel new emotions, they will appear in this yellow tray. They will be in "file-form" with a neat white label.

You walk into your office and bang your hip into the fax machine. The file "Annoyance" appears in your inbox. It's accompanied by "Embarrassment" as your boss comments on your clumsiness. In the kitchen you notice someone made a donut run; you smile. The files "Anticipation" and "Happiness" appear in your inbox. Then, you overhear the back door click shut and the familiar footsteps of that certain someone you've been trying to impress. You hear him walk toward the kitchen and feeling "Frantic," you toss the donut in the trash. The file "Excitement" appears as he rounds the corner. After your conversation with him, the files "Interest," "Curiosity," and "Expectation" have also arrived. You chat with Diane and Cindy on your way back to your desk, and the files "Envy," "Sadness," and "Concern" appear in the yellow tray.

As you sit back down to actually eat a donut, you glance over at your inbox. It's full again. You sigh and begin flipping through the files. You notice several are unlabeled. These are the feelings you were not aware of, feelings you must read in order to label. Will you look them over? Maybe you don't have time.

What do you do with these files? Do you let them just stack up and clutter your work space? Do you work on top of them (feeling without understanding, reacting without understanding)? Do you deny the presence of the files by stuffing them haphazardly in drawers or under your desk? Do you shred them?

Do you deny that you actively invited several of those files into your inbox, ignoring the fact that you asked Cindy about her new car even though you've been eyeing it for a week? Do you refuse to acknowledge your part in waiting, straining even, to identify "his" footsteps? Do you walk away from the desk, quit your job, and pretend it was the job that created the emotional buildup?

The way we interact with our emotions determines our emotional intelligence. We get to choose what emotions we receive, which we fight, which we turn away, and which we ignore. We are "very active in inviting, allowing, and handling" our emotions.[63]

Our minds are part of the filing system, helping us know which feelings to accept and which to turn away. When I feel the desire to flirt with a man I've just met, those are my emotions tugging at my soul. I may feel like lowering my eyes or smiling a little extra warmly, and then I become conscious of my desire (a consistent inclination) to be faithful to my husband. I can choose to file "Greed for Male Attention" or "Longing to Flirt" into the drawer of "Emotions to Meditate on Later" and move out of the way of temptation. I'm asking the emotions to play second fiddle to my desires and beliefs. It is not some newfangled psychological idea. David did just this in Psalm 4:4: "Tremble [with anger or fear] and do not sin." He says it's okay to feel as long as your emotions are guided by you. Then he says, "Meditate

[Speak] in your heart upon your bed, and be still." He chooses to be still in the red light of his emotion.

I'm slowly working out a filing system to be responsible, aware, and intentional about my emotional life. It's a process that means we need to spend time thinking over our feelings, wondering what triggered them, and asking God to change us. It's his business to change my emotions; it's my business to give them to him to change. He and I have to have regular meetings about my inbox.

Emotions indicate something much like an indicator light on our car's dash. A blinking light means something significant is going on under the hood. If you know your car, you know what's wrong just by seeing the light. If you know your soul, you know what's going on in your soul when you see the flashing light of envy, anger, or fear. And as you study your emotions, you learn that some emotions, like anger, are secondary, that they indicate something deeper is wrong. It's up to you to find soul space to think and ask the Spirit of God to help.

Women have a chance to get really good at knowing these indicator lights. If you have emotional intelligence, you can love God with, not in spite of, your emotions. We can take the overflowing inbox and order it so that others see a woman of strength and passion, making God known on earth. Instead of seeing emotions as an inconvenient hurdle, we can say, "This is how God enjoys and orders emotions."

Resemblance #6: Cultivation

I have often heard that women are natural nurturers. The root word for nurture means to nourish or sustain — the Latin *nutrire*, "to suckle." But I think the word "nurture" is rather narrow; it sounds like something I won't do well until I have a baby and can nurse. Nurturing, in this sense, can tend to cut off the women who are young, women who don't have children, women who are unmarried, women whose children don't need nurturing anymore, and women who aren't the nurturing types.

Nurturing is just a sliver of the resourceful, initiating abilities that women give the world. Our femininity is something beyond baby bearing. We ought not require a woman to bear a child or nurse the little one to prove her womanhood. If we do, then millions of women are sidelined, excluded, and even worse, they feel like God has no room for them.

One caveat: I've never birthed a child. I've only whelped a pack of Corgi puppies. If God gives me the delight of a baby, my views about the significance or symbolism of motherhood may very well flex and grow. Nevertheless, the capacity of our bodies to have babies is not a unique gift. Birthing and milk making does not make us uniquely human, much less feminine. All mammals bear and nurse children, so to associate a woman's uniqueness with her mammalian qualities is hardly a compliment to her humanity. We are uniquely female in the way our souls respond to lactating, nursing, weaning, and raising children. In this way, we show our feminine souls, but not in our birthing or nursing abilities alone.[64] Our soul's femininity must be something Eve was created with before she was dubbed "Mother of All the Living," before Cain or Able were a twinkle in her eye.[65]

Let's use a new word like "cultivation."[66] Cultivation allows me to think more broadly. Cultivate means (1) to improve and prepare (land), as by plowing or fertilizing, for raising crops; till; (2) to loosen or dig (soil) around growing plants; (3) to grow or tend (a plant or crop); (4) to promote the growth of; (5) to nurture, foster; (6) to form and refine, as by education.[67]

Cultivation means that I put my sweat and blood, ideas and plans, into something. Cultivate means to order, to give, to grow, to lead, to promote. Cultivation makes me think of what mothers do with their children's minds and abilities, what women do at work, what women do with their husbands, in their churches, in their homes. And what women do in their souls.

For the cultivating woman, the world is our garden, a garden that we work and till. We tend people. Edith Stein said, "The woman's soul is ... fashioned as a shelter in which other souls may unfold."[68] We might be a social organizer, an administrator, or a leader, but we are tending the souls around us. It's all over our language, as in at**tend** or at**ten**tion or ex**tend** or **tend**erness. My friend Di ex**tend**s her friendship with long, sporadic, newsy emails just to keep me up on her mind's musings. My aunt listens for hours offering **tend**er, nonintrusive advice. My counselor pays at**ten**tion to the false ideas in my mind. My sister ex**tend**s herself to make gifts like a mug with my name on it. My mother at**ten**tively notices my low days. My grandmother **tend**ed my creativity and grew it into gardening. My other grandmother ex**tend**s herself to water my plants. Cultivating women do this tending again and again, consistently, practically working, naturally building other people—a long cultivation in the same direction.

We tend our bodies. Teenage girls will often turn their soul toward cultivating their appearance, tending their style. Beth Moore jokingly says that when she was a teen, she was convinced her spiritual gift was accessorizing. Now she uses the skill of cultivating herself to build up other women's souls. It's the same gift, but oriented in a different direction.

We tend the space around us. You might use cultivation to make beauty, order, and comfort. I buy colorful rugs for my kitchen, my aunt hangs pictures of the Eiffel Tower. My counselor has potpourri and flowery wallpaper in her waiting room. None are *the* feminine thing to do. We cultivate in different ways because we have unique souls. If you are a woman who has this ability, you will cultivate with every capacity (spirit, mind, will, desire, and feeling).

We will have desires to cultivate as we are best capable: to care, feed, clothe, warm, and satisfy. We will think on different ways to comfort people and beautify a space. We will believe that cultivating others is worth inconveniencing ourselves, and we'll schedule accordingly.

We'll cultivate in our offices, in court, in the classroom, in the church, and in government. We will create an atmosphere of home (it's as varied as the many different women there are) wherever we go.

In her remarkable World War II memoir, *The Hiding Place*, Corrie ten Boom describes passing her sister Betsie's cell in a German prison. Gleaming between the bars was her sister's golden hair framed by two brightly colored scarves—the ones Betsie had been wearing the night of their arrest. They were pinned against the scarred walls of her prison. She had cultivated beauty even in a prison cell. The Nazis couldn't stamp that out of her soul.

I realize men can do interior decorating. We've chosen a clever man to help us with items in our home. He does his job quite well. Men do cultivating well (especially when they're in love). Cultivation flames up brilliantly in my husband around my birthday. Men can cook, too, of course. Men claim to be the world's best chefs (or so I've been repeatedly, discouragingly reminded). But even if these men cook every meal for their family, I'm not certain that cooking meals is the same as that regular, comprehensive, multi-directed, ceaselessly intentional cultivation that women offer.[69]

The Femininity behind the Fashion

This flexible list of family resemblances helps explain why women's fashion sometimes gets marketed as "soft femininity" and "graceful shapes and whisper-soft fabrics." Intricate and detailed blouses, playful scarves, and transparent camisoles echo externally how some women want to live and move. Some will want to look sensitively aware, as they are in their souls. Other women will want to appear capable of cultivating; they want to be taken seriously as qualified human persons and they will dress accordingly. Other women will want to look vulnerable and playful when they're on a date. Other women will be interdependent, and they will dress more like than unlike their friends.

A pair of high heels could be a sign of a woman's femininity. But too often stilettos reveal a soul that is tippy, uncomfortable, and overly concerned with captivating some glances. It's the trappings, the look of vulnerability too often combined with the powerful stride of a woman who means business. It is still quite appealing to look vulnerable even if you haven't spent energy trying to own your vulnerability.

Fashion femininity is only a glimmer of our soul, and often we try hard to appear different than we are. We can use our bodies to hide ourselves or reveal ourselves. Some of the most revealing clothing has been worn by determinedly closed women. If the more "feminine" styles remind a woman of how she's been exploited for her femininity, then she might firmly refuse to wear a skirt or heels. It may be hard for her to remember that once, a long time ago when clothes weren't necessary, a woman's body echoed her soul's vulnerability. Unless Christ enters our souls, we will wrestle with that soul trait forever.

Discovering Your Femininity

We've run through the colors of natural femininity, specific characteristics that give us, finally, a flexible list of what women's souls are all about. We know that we may have some of them, maybe all of them. But each of us experiences femininity differently. How we use our natural femininity will depend on which characteristics are natural to us. It will also depend on our family of origin, our birth order, our personality, our resources, our soul's growth — to mention just a few factors. Each woman works out her characteristics depending on how she chooses to use them with her soul. Which characteristics form your natural, God-given womanhood? Which are you using?

- Interwoven with a female body
- Vulnerable
- Interdependent
- Sensitively aware
- Emotionally intelligent
- Cultivator

One way to determine what is natural to you is to take inventory of each soul capacity. What do you think and believe when you are alone? What consumes your imagination? What were your desires as a child, what forms your predominate desires now? What emotions do you experience more often than others? What choices have you made that you are proud of? Where has your spirit seen truth in yourself?

Ask God's Spirit to guide you into truth about your womanhood. Edith Stein writes, "Whatever enters the soul, and whatever leaves it is in a way impregnated by ... individuality. Even grace is received by each soul in its own particular way."[70] May her words speak freedom into your growth with God to discover and own your womanhood.

Natural Tomatoes

I've bought enough hothouse tomatoes and sliced their tough skin, watching their bleary, watery juice leak out a faint pink color, that I forget how tomatoes are supposed to look. Last summer, I learned that tomatoes bleed a dark red, that their juice can dye things. My husband picked two heirloom tomatoes from the backyard, and when he sliced them, the juice dribbled on our white kitchen towel. I just stared at it. It looked like someone had bled on it. It was deep and pulpy and crimson. *Is that normal?* I wondered. *It looks much too good to be normal.*

A woman who is free and enjoying her natural femininity may not be the normal woman we're expecting. She may have a short haircut. She may be a lawyer with two children. She may be a single pastor, but in her soul, she is woman—deep, rich, essential, earthy, feminine.[71] It might shock us, but we'll have to sigh, marvel, and maybe expand our definition of womanhood.

Soul Care

1. How is a family resemblance list different from most lists you've found for femininity?

2. Are there any resemblances you think should be added to this list?

3. Which resemblances are natural to you? How do you know?

4. If you are interdependent, how might the discipline of solitude help you?

5. Are you tempted to think that if you don't own all resemblances, you are not fully feminine? What does that say about yourself? What does that say about the way you will judge the women who have less than you?

6. Do you value sensitivity?

7. What does your current emotional filing system look like? Describe or sketch it.

8. How are cultivation and nurturing similar and different?

9. Have you felt silenced in one resemblance? Is something within your soul clamoring to be let out?

10. Read Job 19:25–26. Do you think your femininity is something about you that you keep, even when your body is gone? In other words, do you think you will interact with God in heaven as a woman, or as an androgynous soul?

11. Read Luke 10:34–38. Does Jesus mean our resurrected bodies will have no gender, or that we will no longer participate in the exclusive institution of marriage?

12. In preparation for the next chapter:
    - List some character traits about God that remind you of yourself.
    - Look up Isaiah 49:15–16; 66:12–13; and Matthew 23:37 and compare God's desires to your own. What does this tell you about God's soul?

finding the feminine in the sacred

The archetype and ultimate origin of every woman is God.

Getrud von le Fort

One evening at a college in the Midwest, I spoke to a group of females on how women are made in God's image.[1] One eager woman with sparkling blue eyes came up to talk to me afterward. She was curious about 1 Corinthians 11:7, a much used and abused passage that reads, "For a man ought not to have his head covered, since he is the image and glory of God; but the woman is the glory of man."

She wanted to know if she needed a husband to glorify God. I pointed to my husband, Dale, who was sitting in the auditorium, discussing more questions with a group of girls. I explained that Dale is representing God to the girls, and each of them is representing God back to him. They don't need to be married to do that. Whenever we interact with any man—friend, father, brother, boyfriend, or husband—we show God on earth.

"So I don't need a husband to be made in God's image?" This young woman was staring at me intently, as if her identity depended on the answer.

Inwardly I shuddered that somehow she was living in that fear. I shook my head. "No, you don't need a husband. You show God's image all the time."

Wanting a Woman

God wanted a woman to help show his image on earth. Adam wasn't enough to fulfill the call and destiny of humanity. He was working away, subduing, but he wasn't filling and multiplying or fully representing. So God splashed more of his triune image on this planet in the form of Woman.

As women, you and I show the world more about God than a wild buck or the Amazon River, more than a creeping caterpillar or a rock. Something about the woman God created us to be shows the world more about his image. One nineteenth-century philosopher got the idea of how much women can offer the world about God:

> There are thus two human souls, that is a masculine soul and a feminine soul. Thus, woman not only has a soul ... but she has a soul essentially different from ours, a soul which is the inverse of ours, inverse and complementary. *Different* in mind and heart, *different* in imagination and character, intimately and essentially different, woman brings us a new spiritual world and not only a more or less watered down re-edition of the spiritual world of man.[2]

Women are hungry to know how we can offer something spiritual to the world. It is vital that we direct our study to our Maker, the triune God who holds all good masculine and feminine attributes in his being. Natural femininity is not created to be naturally weak, manipulative, or controlling. The woman's soul was not made to be any of these things because we were made to reflect God. Natural masculinity is not overbearing, arrogant, clueless, emotionally disconnected, or vicious, because men also reflect God. Neither masculinity nor femininity needs to be permanently warped, not if we look to our God, the archetype from which our souls were made.

Can God Be Male?

The way we view God will determine what we think about being his image bearer. If God is male, then women don't really show God as well as men. The International Council for Gender Studies claims that men "share masculinity with God." They say that God is male because God is never "she" in Scripture. If the fatherhood of God, or the masculine pronouns indicate an essential maleness of our deity, then where does that leave women? God's maleness puts men closer to God's image than women, making men intrinsically more valuable, even better because of their sex, not because of Christ's work in their lives.

Like most people, I usually think of God as male. I imagine him with a beard or as the God-Man Jesus, probably because of the decades of indoctrination I received from pictures in flannel graph presentations, religious paintings, and cartoon children's stories. It is only lately that I've wondered at the ramifications this vision has had on my identity. I've realized my Sunday school training in the maleness of God was incomplete. Before anyone gets worried, I do not think simply calling God "she" will solve this problem. But I do think that we need to take time to know what we mean when we call God "he."

Much language is figurative when we speak about God. The fatherhood of God is metaphorical as is the sonhood of Jesus. God chose "Father" and "Son" as names for himself. These names offer good pictures, but they do not prove that God is male. I am not saying the metaphor isn't meaningful or literal. The metaphor is real: God is Father in that he literally cares for us with attention and delight. God is Father in that he literally adopted us, and we really are his children now. God is Father in that he is our authority and guide, but it is the metaphor that is masculine, not God.[3] God is more Father than any father on earth could be.

God as Father is not the same as saying God is male. As good as the picture is, God the Father is still a picture. There are some ways the metaphor cannot be literal. God the Father did not create us by impregnating a woman (as Mormons believe), nor did God the Father hang out by himself and then create the Son (as Jehovah's Witnesses believe). The Father is not older than the Son.

The Son of God never began to exist, like most fathers' sons. John says the Logos "was in the beginning with God."[4] Later on, the Logos "became flesh and dwelt among us."[5] But the birth of Jesus did not begin the life of the Son; he was always Logos, with the Father, hanging stars in place, throwing planets into orbit, and co-laboring with the Spirit.

The metaphor touches reality in that Jesus is literally dependent upon the Father for his identity, like a child upon his parents. Theologically Jesus is eternally begotten, not made. His relationship with the Father is as tightly interwoven as parent-child. Like a father gives his genes to his son, so do the Father and Son share the same substance, the same immaterial stuff. The Son is not younger, nor does the Father hold the keys of the kingdom or authority any more than the Son. As Jesus said before he ascended, "All authority has been given to Me in heaven and on earth."[6]

He Is God

God is not material. He doesn't have body parts. Of course, in keeping with gendered souls, God could have a male soul. But if God were a male soul, then females are not created in his image, not as much as males. To think of God in terms of sex at all is a dead end.[7]

"Watch yourselves carefully, since you did not see any form on the day the LORD spoke to you, . . . so that you do not act corruptly and make a graven image for yourselves in the form of any figure, the likeness of male or female" (Deut. 4:15 – 16).

We refer to God as "he" for several reasons: the Son chose to take a male body, Jesus refers to himself as "Son of Man" in the Gospels, and while God uses both masculine and feminine metaphors to describe himself, he never calls himself Mother.[8] Still, the use of "he" shouldn't discourage women from finding the root of their femininity in God. If we make God into a male, then we miss some of the feminine things God does. "For by Him all things were created, both in the heavens and on earth, visible [bodies] and invisible [souls] . . . all things have been created through Him and for Him."[9] The God of the Scriptures put himself into woman. I am so thankful for his confirmation of that in Genesis 1:27: "So God created human beings in his own image, in the image of God he created them; male and female he created them" (TNIV). God fashioned us in his image; we have his fingerprint on our bodies and his breath in our souls. Women, no more and no less than men, are living cameos of God.

One of my favorite psalms is part of the Songs of Ascents collection, sung as the Israelites made their pilgrimages to and from Jerusalem. I imagine them singing this song as they leave the weeks of feasting and resting, or as they gear up with anticipation for reunions with friends and family, as they anticipate the shalom that comes from time with God.

> *Surely I have composed and quieted my soul;*
> *Like a weaned child rests against his mother,*
> *My soul is like a weaned child within me.*[10]

Here, the psalmist uses a picture of the nursing relationship between a mother and her child to describe his — and all of Israel's — relationship to God. God is the mother who weans; they are the children who rest.

But the first time I heard those lines from Psalm 131—I mean, the first time I really heard them, the first time I stopped to think about what they meant—well, I have to admit I was somewhat taken aback.

God as a nursing mother?

Well, yes. It turns out that the psalmist's picture of God as a nursing mother is just one of the feminine metaphors we find in Scripture for God. Now I'm not going to tell you that Jesus was androgynous, or that we should start calling God "she." I'm not claiming that God birthed the world or that the earth is really the body of God. I am not advocating a sort of pantheistic worldview. God's kingliness, his authority, and his separateness as Creator is quite clear in Scripture. I do not think God is needy of us, nor that God is lonely without us. To think that God *needs* is contrary to worshiping a being mighty enough to elicit our adoration. And yet, there is a vital need to see how God claims womanly pictures for himself.

I want to redirect our attention to some of the often overlooked pictures of God in the Bible, and then consider what we can learn about God, and what we can learn about our own feminine souls by considering those pictures.

Lost Biblical Images of God

The Bible is full of different metaphors for God. These metaphors and images help us finite beings grasp some of the characteristics of God. Many of the metaphors, of course, are masculine. God is a shepherd—a metaphor that teaches us that God knows our whereabouts as a shepherd knows his sheep. God is a bridegroom—he is as delighted about his church as a bridegroom is delighted about his bride. God is a warrior—he will fight our battles for us with ferocity and courage.

Other biblical images for God are neither masculine nor feminine. God is a door. God is a cornerstone, a vine. In the gospel of

John, when Jesus tells us that he is the door, it doesn't mean he is *literally* a door. Jesus is instead telling us that he is the way to the Father, the way to eternal life. Similarly, when Jesus says, "I am the vine, you are the branches," he does not mean he is green and twiggy—but he is, very literally, our life source. At the end of Deuteronomy, when he is reminding the people of Israel, once and for all, who God is, Moses uses a whole host of metaphors, some feminine, some masculine: "Ascribe greatness to our God! The Rock!... Is not He your Father who has bought you? He has made you and established you."[11]

God is no less like a rock, stable and mighty, than he is like a Father, adopting Israel, making Israel, establishing Israel. Both metaphors have touching points to reality. And yet God is not like an earthly father who has a birthday, nor is he made out of a mineral compound like a rock. "You neglected the Rock who begot you, And forgot the God who gave you birth."[12] Moses compares God to a rock again, but this time in association with the motherly aspects of birthing. God is like a stable, steadfast mother, birthing Israel, connected to Israel, concerned for the health and growth of Israel.

Isaiah, probably more than any other prophet, proved God's concern with female images. In chapter 42 God says:

I have kept silent for a long time,
I have kept still and restrained Myself.
Now like a woman in labor I will groan,
I will both gasp and pant.[13]

I certainly don't think this image makes him look steady or mighty. It makes him look awfully vulnerable. It makes God sound very, well, feminine.

Last year, I heard an older woman speak about God and gender at the Evangelical Theological Conference. She was a respected professor in a conservative seminary, one that claimed Baptist roots. She knew teaching was a privilege and a responsibility, and she was to show herself worthy—particularly since she was a woman teaching at an institution where most of the teachers were men.

Her session's title was "God and Gender: Is God Male or Female? Both or Neither?" In the middle of her talk, she told a story. One day, she was sitting in her small office reading Isaiah, and she came upon that panting and groaning verse in Isaiah 42:14. It arrested her like it probably did me and you. She stopped and read it again. She sat back, gazing out the window into the blank hallway. No one was in the office except her and the triune God. She started flipping to another passage and read, "Can a woman forget her nursing child and have no compassion on the son of her womb? Even these may forget, but I will not forget you."[14]

She thought about the pictures and felt uncomfortable with them. She turned to one of the last passages in the book.

> "Shall I bring to the point of birth and not give delivery?" says
>   the LORD.
> "Or shall I who gives delivery shut the womb?" says your God.
> "Be joyful with Jerusalem and rejoice for her, all you who love
>   her;
> Be exceedingly glad with her, all you who mourn over her,
> That you may nurse and be satisfied with her comforting
>   breasts,
> That you may suck and be delighted with her bountiful
>   bosom."
> For thus says the LORD, "... And you will be nursed, you will be
>   carried on the hip and fondled on the knees.
> "As one whom his mother comforts, so I will comfort you."[15]

Slowly, she turned the pages back to Isaiah 42:14, and leaning back into her chair, she pulled the Bible close to her and read aloud and slowly: "Like a woman in labor I will groan, I will both gasp and pant." What did this mean? Suddenly, there in her office, the God of

Isaiah ceased to be an abstraction. God became very, very personal, and the professor knew God was moving in her spirit. She knew she was being shown something about God that she had not been willing to accept before.

God was in pain for Israel. God writhed in labor pains for Israel. But it wasn't just for Israel. Slowly she said, "God writhed in labor pains for ... me." She began to weep, and out of her tears she barely whispered, "She ... writhed in labor pains for me." Weeping alone in her office, this seminary professor was not alone, the persons of Father, Son, and Holy Spirit held her as she, like Isaiah, fell undone in the presence of God.

The next day, she prepared an unusual lecture for her class. She told them that she had experienced God the night before, and that out of this experience she loved God more, she understood God's tenderness for her more, and she was able to worship and serve him with might and intensity.

She read the passages in Isaiah to her class. Some women in the class cried as they saw God afresh. And men cried too as they saw more of God, less of man. And the class breathed together in worship as they pressed on to know God.

What am I saying? Not that God is our mother or that we should call God "she" or that we should pray, "Mother God."[16] The predominant title in Scripture, one Jesus uses, is "Daddy" or *Abba*." For those reasons, "Father" has been the dominant language the church uses when speaking of or addressing the first person of the Trinity.[17]

But that doesn't mean God does not mother us. We can thank God for mothering us, for nursing us, for laboring over us. To make our verbs say what our nouns cannot say. God mothers us better than any earthly mother. We can thank God for rebirthing us, for that is what "born again" means — the labor of God for us in the life, death, and resurrection of Christ.

We can glorify him for working hard like a mother to see godliness grow in us. He is working within, without, in heaven, and on earth, mothering us through the sanctification process. Jesus called it being *born* of water and the Spirit. In Romans 8 we have all three persons of the Trinity working with us: "the Spirit Himself intercedes for us," Christ "intercedes for the saints according to the will of God," and the Father "foreknows, predestines and conforms us to the image of His Son." The picture could not be more apt.

Debbie Blue, pastor and mother of two, writes that God is not "the impassive patriarch who demands specific sorts of actions before he'll allow people any sort of intimacy, before he'll allow people to be close to him … Scripture really paints such an entirely different picture. Like God birthing us. That's sort of intimate from the get go."[18] The metaphor is feminine, but God is not. Jesus provides a picture of God as the birther, and if nothing else, this metaphor can help us get rid of that awful picture of God as some old man in the sky who is über-masculine — complete with white beard and a sin-sniffing personality. There is no such old man God, nor is there a harlequin romancing, softly permed Jesus, nor is God a woman. We need to conceive of God without conjuring up goofy, tacky pictures, which is why we need God's Word. He balances our view with good masculine and feminine pictures, so we remember both sets of characteristics come from the Godhead.

The birthing actions in Isaiah are a foreshadowing of what Christ came to offer — rebirth. This is an experience women can help us name and more fully understand. God does indeed groan for us as a laboring mother groans.[19] God sustains us as a nursing mother sustains her helpless baby, keeping us nourished and outfitted.[20] God works to give us new, abundant life.[21] God births us into that second life, life from his labor.

The Bible's feminine language for God makes a lot of people nervous. So nervous that we tend to ignore it completely. (When was the last time you heard a sermon that addressed God suckling us?) We are too quickly satisfied with our man-made ideas of God, refusing to let Scripture re-center us.

To do so — to ignore the Bible's feminine imagery for God — is disastrous, for at least two reasons. First, it effectively erases part of Scripture. Second, it erases a lot of women, both women inside and outside the church.

We need to balance all the "God is male" imagery in our prayers and sermons, small groups and songs. We should of course continue to use "Father" language as our primary way of discussing God, and we should continue to use other masculine imagery that comes from Scripture. But we need to integrate the Bible's feminine language into our songs and sermons and prayers too. If anyone at church finds such pictures beneath them, doesn't this say more about their prejudice against women than their knowledge of God? The language we use in the church should reflect *all* the metaphors the Bible offers us for God. It should also reflect the full image of God, which was made as woman and man. Let us acknowledge the feminine things God does. Let us thank God for birthing Israel, for nursing us, for weaning us, for laboring over us. All of these, after all, are verbs that God the Father chose.

Hearing the Christian Feminists

We need to listen to women who want to call God "Mother" and find out why. We must end our diatribe of calling them overreacting, oversensitive, angry, or male-hating feminists. We might offer these women the feminine attributes of God so they might rediscover the masculinity of God, as well.[22] We must face them as real persons who may struggle and even hate the idea of God as Father, but for good reasons. We might listen to them charitably and generously to learn what their scars look like, to find out what they fear. Jesus, I think, would have listened with unshockable, compassionate, I-have-all-the-time-in-the-world-for-you attention. He would have looked beyond the posturing and seen the wounds many of these women carry. We need to ask about their bleeding. We need to pause in the middle of our crowded rooms and let our church programs be checked by women with hurts and women with questions.[23] For this is what Christ did. We need to consider how Jesus wants to heal them, and us.

What We Learn

I can look at a rock and find things about God because rocks always obey their nature. When God says, "I am a Rock," it's a good, stable metaphor. Thousands of years later, it still communicates well.

When I look at my dad, I know there are some ways he is like my heavenly Dad. The metaphor helps me see God's personality: God cares for me, as my dad does; God wants what's best for me, as my dad does.

But, of course, my dad is a fallen human, so the metaphor breaks down a bit. If my dad belittles me, I will struggle to remember that God does not. But that seeming limitation is part of the beauty of metaphors. My earthly dad can teach me some things about God, but at the same time, my heavenly Dad corrects my earthly dad and gives me a better picture of what true fatherhood looks like. The metaphor, in other words, works in two directions.[24] I know some things about God because I know my dad, and I know what my dad should be because I know God.

We can say the same thing about God and women — we learn more about God when we read Isaiah's description of God as a nursing mother, because we have seen women carefully feed their babies. But by reflecting on the nature of God, we also learn a lot about how we as women should strive to be. For the rest of this chapter, I want to look closely at three ways our femininity was forged from God's character: God is a cultivator; God is interdependent; and God is sensitively aware, as are women. By reflecting on these characteristics of God, we can learn more about our femininity, and by reflecting on our lives as women, we might deepen our understanding of God.

El Shaddai: The Great Cultivator

In Sunday school, I was taught that *El* means God and *Shaddai* means Almighty. But the title means more than "All-powerful One." The first time God promises to make Abram fruitful, he identifies himself as *El Shaddai*. Job, a contemporary of Abram, says it is the breath of *El Shaddai* that gives him life.[25] Isaac blesses Jacob with *El Shaddai's* blessing to make him fruitful.[26] When Israel blesses Joseph, he chooses a blessing of *El Shaddai*.[27] A Hebrew lexicon will show you that *Shaddai* comes from the root *shad*, which means "female breast," or "of woman," or "of mother."[28] One of the core names of God is rooted in a womanly activity. God is revealing that he can accurately be called one who nurses, who makes fruitful, who sustains. God is like a mother, like a woman. As *El Shaddai* sustains all aspects of life, he does it with all-mighty energy: cultivating the blessings, cultivating the curses, cultivating fertility, and cultivating people.

God is like mothers, but mothers are also like God. Mothers cultivate life like *El Shaddai*. In this metaphor, women have an experiential edge over men, our bodies are made with specific capacities for fertility and life giving. As friends of mine have explained, the building and growing of life in their wombs is unlike anything they've known. This experience is something that God's soul knows in a more profound way. He doesn't birth Adam and Eve; he created them *ex nihilo*, but God says the intimacy he has with all humans is more like a woman with her baby, than a man with his baby. Men do not have the chance to feel their baby's life unfolding and growing.

From the very first pages in Genesis, God cultivates life in other ways. He prepared the first garden specifically for his two image bearers and then handed them the keys. He wanted them to cultivate the land that he had already cultivated for them. And God asked them to work with each other, having already begun a relationship with each of them. When they blew it, he kept cultivating. We botched up Eden, so he's cultivating another place for us: "In My Father's house are many dwelling places ... I go to prepare a place for you."[29]

God's constant efforts to make a place for us remind me of the women in my life: My Aunt Barb who lives in Pebble Beach always sits me in the same special spot at her breakfast nook, my grandmother who made "lechita," a glass of warm milk and molasses in the evenings, my other grandmother who made me pearl tea (warm milk with sugar), and my mother who found the biggest and juiciest strawberries for me as a child. All these women bring me help and nourishment. These women are pictures of God to me. Just as these women are always tending, so God is tending each of us.

Perhaps the single best example of sustained, systematic, and comprehensive cultivation is the Law. God took it upon himself to work out a civilizing program for humans. His covenant with Israel was meant to guide them through life in a fallen world. The Law was all about helping Israel find and sustain the good life through moral, civil, and ceremonial law. God even added a detailed description of his tabernacle, including interior decorating specifications for colors, textiles, dimensions, and metallurgy. He educated his people in beauty, in love, in faithfulness. Chapter after chapter, God tirelessly cultivated the nomads of Jacob, much like many women do today in all jobs: teaching, mothering, administrating, debating, speaking.

God makes Israel his people by tending and softening their stiff necks, working balm into their muscles until they rest upon him. Jesus longed to do precisely the same thing. "How often I wanted to gather your children together, just as a hen gathers her brood under her wings, and you would not have it!"[30] He is still saying to us, "Come ... all who are weary and heavy-laden, and I will give you rest. Take My yoke, my law, my ways, my life upon you and learn from

Me, for I am gentle and careful and sensitive with you. And you will find rest for your souls."[31]

Why the Trinity Dignifies Women

Christianity dignifies interdependence. It is the only religion that offers interdependence in the very nature of God. God is three in one, and since he is triune, God is the most complete example of an interdependent being. His identity is forged from his intimacy more than the most interdependent, connected-knowing woman. When Jesus was on earth, he explained that he was connected to the Father, and the Spirit was connected to him in an interdependence that has required a doctrine as complicated and profound as the Trinity to explain. The Trinity, historically, solves the confusion of how God is Spirit and Son and Father, distinct persons and yet one essence.[32]

To understand how the Trinity works, we must start with love. Love is perhaps the most praised and universal value in all religions. The final anthem in Broadway's fabulous remake of Victor Hugo's book *Les Miserables* rings true: "To love another person is to see the face of God." We expect God to be the quintessence of love.

Imagine God before he created. There are no other beings about, no angels, definitely no demons, only him. Now, if God were single, only one, he could not love. He would only be able to love himself, which we don't really think of as love. It's more like narcissism. Without another being, God could not show love. He wouldn't be able to sacrifice for another, because there is no other being around for which he might sacrifice. God would be unable to show the most significant of all the virtues. He would actually need to create someone so he could love. But if God needs, then he's not really God; he's a deficient, dependent being.

But if God were somehow more than one, he wouldn't have that problem. Maybe God is two, then he could love and sacrifice for the other without leaving the Godhead. But even two isn't quite enough to really show love. Sure, love means sacrifice, willing another's good, but it also means working with another for the benefit of a third party. God must surely be able to show that cooperative love that parents know about, the love that springs out of working together, like planning a birthday party or saving up money for a first family vacation. To be unrestricted in his loving, God would need to be at least three, and then two could cooperate for the benefit of the third.[33]

According to the historic teachings of the church, that is precisely the type of God who exists. God was, is, and will always be three persons. Christian theologians say that if God exists, he must be a Trinity: one divinity, the three persons all divine.

The Trinity embodies interdependence. Each member's identity emerges out of their intimacy. We identify each member of the Trinity because of their relationship to each other. Father comes out of his relationship with his Son. Spirit is eternally "proceeding," as the Athanasian Creed says, from Father and Son together. In their work on earth, the Father and Son rely on the Spirit's power to work in the souls of humans.[34] Even Jesus relied on the Spirit to give him supernatural knowledge.[35] The members of the Trinity have knowledge of themselves and one another because they are as fully connected as any beings could be. They know everything, including each other's minds, emotions, wills. Their unity of knowledge, unity of intimacy, and unity of action make them interdependent in every decision that is made. One decision on the part of the Son emptying himself to become a man ripples along the coursing life of the Godhead: the Father gives, the Spirit overshadows, and the Logos takes on flesh.[36] This interconnected life is where women can look to find how good interdependence can be.

Women can root their interdependence in the nature of the Christian God. We don't need leverage from matriarchal societies, or psychological studies to prove that we are valuable. For when women depend on each other, we are smaller pictures of the Trinity. The

Father depends on the Son to give himself up: "For this reason the Father loves Me, because I lay down My life so that I may take it again."[37] The Son depends on the Father to raise him: "But God raised Him up again, putting an end to the agony [or birth pangs] of death."[38] And the Father and Son depend on the Spirit to abide with us: "I will ask the Father, and He will give you another Helper, that He may be with you forever."[39]

If we ever wonder if our interdependence is essentially weakness, we need only look to God. In him we see identity and intimacy linked together and no shadow of frailty in him. We need to root ourselves in God's image. When women are interdependent, they show a godly attribute for earth to see. We are like God when we engage in identity-making relationships. Eve is like God in that she knew life in relationship and love; she was never a lone human. Like God, Eve experienced identity with another who was equal to her.

Sensitive Awareness in God

When Eve used her dominion to set up her own ideas, God's sensitivity came out in bold relief. God blessed her in the midst of his curse, making the one who initiated disobedience also the initiator of redemption. She would bear the curse and the solution.[40] In *Paradise Lost*, John Milton gives Eve these words to say: "to me reproach / Rather belongs, distrust and all dispraise; / But infinite in pardon was my Judge, / That I who first brought Death on all, am favored to be / The source of life."[41] This is the first picture of grace in Scripture, and it begins in the way God judges his female image bearer.

The God who cursed Eve is also the God who chose Mary. He was providing the supporting evidence for his original thesis — that a woman would be pivotal in undoing what was done. I am not suggesting that Mary worked hard and earned this position. Mary was full of grace because God graced her. Mary's acceptance was full of effort, though she never acted as if she'd earned it. She did not say,

"Well, yes, I think I've been working awfully hard to prove how excellent a mother I'd be. Glad you agree!" The Virgin Mary chose to accept the life of shame and misunderstanding instead of blissful, glowing union with Joseph. Surely with much effort she said, "May it be done to me according to your word." And she prepared herself with a retreat of three months with one of her dear friends. Her efforts accompanied the first steps of God's incarnation. Her efforts crowned the disgrace of Eve with the willing grace of a young woman's willing submission. Her submission, contrary to the kind preached in most churches, began with questions and ends with her sacrifice. The seed of the Woman would crush the Serpent's head.

Mary, the young and vulnerable, is the first human participant to join Christ in crushing the Evil One. Perhaps Satan's sentiments were much like the Wicked Witch in her famous melting scene: "What a world, what a world. Who would have thought a good little girl like you could destroy all my beautiful wickedness." I see God's sensitivity all over this tremendous drama by casting his supporting lead as a young, unmarried female.

Learning from Women

If we really believed women manifest God as much as men, we might be more willing to let women teach on passages of Scripture. We might ask a mother to preach on what "born again" has meant in her life. We might ask a female athlete to comment on Jael, who murdered Sisera in Judges. We might ask an unmarried woman with the gift of teaching to speak about Anna, the prophetess who met the baby Jesus in the temple. We might invite women in politics or widows who are now remarried to share their thoughts on the passage in 1 Samuel 25 where Abigail acts as diplomat, loses her husband, and promptly remarries David. We might watch mothers to see how they love their children. We might call them godly, meaning that they are showing the world what God is like as poignantly and importantly as a father. We also might be more careful to ascribe feminine verbs to God, since he has done so himself. If we did, we might see how each woman, like each man, is a reflection of something different and awe inspiring in God.

Soul Care

1. Does it seem strange, inappropriate, or degrading for God to be feminine?

2. What beliefs do you have about God's masculinity?

3. How did you feel when you read "She writhed in pain for me"?

4. How have you experienced God's interdependence, sensitive awareness, or cultivation in your life?

5. Pray for a new perspective, "Lord, teach me the value you have for my femininity. I want to see myself as you see me. I want to know the shapes you have carved into my soul, the things in me that show you better on earth. Are there places in me I have hidden? Is there something good in me that I am embarrassed to be? Make me confident to be more of you on earth."

seven

frailty, thy name is woman

Many women have more power than they recognize, and they're very hesitant to use it, for they fear they won't be loved.

Patricia Schroeder

t was evening when we walked onto the college track, our old running shoes ricocheting off the bouncy, synthetic material. I heard, rather than saw, my husband keep stride with me. We ran silently, mulling over the last few moments' conversation.

On the way to the track, we ran into an old friend and his new girlfriend. We engaged in a typical first-time meeting, full of nervous laughter. I felt her watching my movements, scrutinizing my features and responses. She was nervous and I was trying not to be. And in trying to impress her and him, I ended up being rather silly and even mean. I scolded my husband, an activity I despise in other wives and in myself. Dale had evenly replied to my scolding, "Why don't you let me take care of myself?"

I flounced out of the awkward moment and into the cool air. I think the air could have helped me calm down, but I didn't let it. I wanted to be mad at him. My will steered my mind back to the conversation, and I began rehashing the appropriate blame—all his, none mine. As our feet hit the track, I could only think of how mean he was.

We finished the first lap in stony silence. Our shadows were cast by the moon shining through a chain-link fence around the track and made me feel chained inside. I felt stuck to pound in sync with my husband—this man I had chosen to be mine. We were chained together on the track, chained to work this out. I willed hot and angry sobs to bubble up into my throat. I let them out in exaggerated, dramatic bursts.

"Are you okay?" Dale asked. I nodded imperceptibly, wanting him to strain in his stride to catch it. He didn't notice so he slowed down and asked more loudly, "Are you okay?" I swung my head up and down in a big, curt nod that was definitely not okay. He was silent. I sped up my pace.

And we kept circling, around and around, broken man and broken woman.

Under my new running shoes and workout clothes, I felt sick. I was afraid that I was everything I hated in other women—the nagging woman; the overbearing, controlling wife; the silent disapproving female; the indirect, passive-aggressor; the manipulative woman. How quickly womanly virtue becomes womanly vice: our interdependence becomes clingy insecurity, our sensitivity becomes entitlement, our emotional intelligence morphs into emotional abuse, our cultivation turns into drippy nagging.[1]

Fallen Femininity

I have one potted star jasmine that requires lots of watering. When I neglect it, the soil pulls away from its terra-cotta pot and transforms from a moist, tender home into a rigid vice. Life-giving material turns into an earthen tomb. It sticks in a clump to the delicate root system, holding water and resources away from the plant. The soil that gave life now sucks the life out.

There are women like that. Women who insist that they are the ones to meet all your needs, sure that they know best, women who cannot let their children grow up or their husband bumble through a new task or their friend make a mistake. Women who insist on helping—even when you want to do it yourself. Women who cannot accept, but must always give.

I detest this quality in other women because I know it lurks within me. My faults don't always look bad—they're often veiled in helpfulness or concern or sacrificial love. My strengths can hurt others when I insist on doing things for them that they can and really ought to do for themselves.

How many women surround themselves with people to love only to cling to those people without respite? Sure my star jasmine needs soil to grow, just like we need people to grow. Sure it feels great to be needed. But are we life-giving? Others must be free to move. When women demand or expect, or cajole and then offer something like the silent treatment when they don't get what they want, we essentially cut off people from our cultivation, sensitivity, interdependence, vulnerability, and emotional intelligence. We set ourselves up as indispensable life givers, and then when questioned or challenged, we may lash out by refusing to offer life. In our networks of interdependence, we can easily cultivate needs that only we can meet. Here are some of those telltale indications that we have cultivated unhealthy dependencies:

- "Did you want something? No, don't get up. I can get it for you."
- "Don't do it like that. Here, give it to me."
- "You always get lost, don't you? Here, give me the map."
- "Let Mommy do it, darling."
- "Did you put them to bed like I do? Are you sure they're okay?"
- "You just needed me to help you out."

My need to be needed makes me force others to depend on me. I'm not talking about healthy interdependence anymore. I'm talking about demanding that we be all goodness, help, and kindness to other people. We don't let them grow, and we are anything but good and kind. This insisting that we be everything can keep a child from growing up, a husband cold and stifled, a relationship stilted, and our own soul a hard, calcified ball of dirt.

When my star jasmine dries out, no matter how long I hold the hose over it, the water will not penetrate the roots. Water beads up on the surface only to spill down the sides and out the bottom. The only way to save the entombed plant is to lug it over to a larger bucket of water and immerse the entire pot and plant in a bath. The water slowly seeps into the earthen tomb, the rigidity relaxes, and in this hour-long baptism, the earth loosens its grip of death.

Over-Cultivated

When I was seven, I planted a row of corn for the family garden. One morning before school, I saw the curved head of a seedling just beginning to break the soil. It looked like agony, trying to push off its heavy mantle, so I helped it a bit. Brushing the soil away, I cleared a path for the sprout to rise up straight and strong.

The next day I went outside to look at the small, sprouted kernel of life. I bent down to inspect it, only to find that all the taut life in the stem had dissolved. The sprout hung limp against the ground, unable to hold itself up. I tried to prop it up with a small twig, but it didn't help. The next day, what with the sun's beating rays, it shriveled up. I had over-helped life. And life died.

Cultivating Dependence

In many churches, single or childless women often feel like they sit one level below the married mothers, those fruitful vines.[2] Blessed are they, perhaps, but what about the unfruitful female? Is her barrenness proof of her inadequacy?

In childhood, I planned and prepared to avoid this singlehood. I would build a network of life, so I could move out of second-class femininity. I would use all my soul's strengths to get a husband. I would grow, cultivate, and lean on him. This life would become — if all things worked out properly — the anchor of my very existence. When someone doubted my value, I could point to my husband and then my brood of kids, not to God whose image I bore. And that, I thought, would make me successful.

By the age of seventeen, I had found the man I was looking for. His was the life I would build on, the life that would bring me more life. I knew where we were headed and the path before me shone clearly, like the fat diamond on my ring finger. Our engagement was a promise to me that our futures would be entwined, that we would have a family, that he could provide for me, and most important, that he needed me.

My soul craved his neediness. I was attracted to his need. He was like Mr. Rochester needing a Jane Eyre. And I basked in his attentions, hungry for his light. I would do anything to show the world the way I met his needs, above and beyond all he could ask or think.

In the name of submission, I bent my young female will to his. I focused all my soul's strengths of sensitivity and emotional intelligence into a laser beam. I lived to please him. I enmeshed myself deep into his gazes, his arms, his goals, his struggles, his failures, his ideas, his worries. And I was praised for it — by admiring girlfriends, by members of my church, by his family and his friends. I gave in to his obsession with all the other men I had dated, giving him details that he should not have bothered with, much less cross-examined me over.

I ignored the emotional alarm flashing in my soul and stuffed down the radar detection that he was obsessing over my past. Instead I chose to be secretly delighted in his jealousy, glad that he needed me so desperately. Even when I wished he would trust me more, I was glad that he craved my purity so voraciously. I wanted to prove myself worthy of his love, and when I looked into his fantastic eyes, I knew that there was no other man I wanted to please.

For three solid years, I spent my energy on him, trying to prove the faithfulness and dedication of my love. I desired his desire, more than I desired his good. So I worked overtime to feed the demands he made on me, to prove how loyal I was. I gave up bits of my mind to please him. In the name of submission, I learned deceit. In the name of romance, I gave up responsibility to my soul.

I've since learned how often women tell themselves these sorts of lies, creating a halo of bright, naive blindness. We cut ourselves off from our mind's ability to honestly reason and feel. We decide that we need the man to prove something; to remind ourselves, the world, the Serpent, and the women around us, that we are not inadequate. And we twist our natural gifts. Every naturally feminine characteristic can be twisted into a fallen one. Those near us feel suffocated, gasping for water, for air, for the Spirit of God's piercing baptism of light. In our desire to be valuable, we may lose the very man we were counting on to give us value, as I did. And then, we might learn what it means to be wanted. We might find that God doesn't require we prove ourselves. In the aftermath of my broken engagement, God whispered in that clear, calm voice, "I want you, Jonalyn, even if this man does not."

Female Wounds

This insight from *Seinfeld*:

Elaine: "Why do guys think wedgies are fun?"
George: "Well, what do girls do for fun?"
Elaine: "We just make fun of a girl behind her back until she develops an eating disorder."

When women fight, we dig deep; of course, men can too. It is a skill that most women hate in fellow females because they hate it in themselves. The more sensitive and emotionally intelligent you are, the more you can subtly dish it out. Like the princess, I can feel the pea in my bed, even if it's buried under twenty mattresses.

And when I've wanted to hurt another princess, I'd put a miniscule bump in her bed, too small for anyone else to notice. She'd wake up black and blue, and she'd know who did it. The pea comes in various forms. I might withhold eye contact or let the silence sit icily in the room. I could drop my eyes to the ground and answer in monosyllables. I might stiffen my back and close off my body. I'd rigidly open a book I care nothing about. I could stare. I might share the detail that I know makes her envious. I'd feign innocence. I'd apologize profusely, but only because I'm more preoccupied with appearing concerned than with being concerned. I would widen my eyes in disapproval or drop them in disgust. I would cultivate interest in her man and pretend fascination in his job because I knew I could hold his attention with my questions. I'd smile coquettishly at the man who walks past, hoping my husband won't notice that I notice that he's noticing me. Then I'd deny it when he does.

When we want to hurt someone, we know the string to pluck. We know the vulnerable spots to gash. We prey on women's weakness, as men do, too, but in other ways. Our interdependence and sensitive awareness become our swords to poke people, like the women warriors in another one of Baum's *Oz* books who hide glittering knitting needles in their hair to stab their enemies.[3] The very marks of our femininity turn into weapons.

We cultivate demands and nurse them with things like, "If he loved me, he would remember to do that." "If she really cared, she would have planned my birthday better." "If he wanted the date to go smoothly, why didn't he look up directions?" "If she really wasn't mad at me, she'd call me back sooner!" "She forgot to invite me on purpose." "I won't smile or even look at her because she . . ." We can concoct venom so powerful that it poisons our soul's feminine strengths.

And when we get really hurt, all we want is to hurt back. I have wanted to hurt my husband as much as I've perceived he wanted to hurt me (usually he doesn't realize he's hurt me). I've heard other women say the same. "I just want to make him suffer like I'm suffering." I know very few men who feel that they want to hurt those they love. I'm not saying men don't wound others, but they often wound without realizing it.

Every painful experience we know of our femininity gets stored up in our souls as evidence for not believing in woman. We stop trusting women, because we know our own woman's soul so well.

Distancing Ourselves from Women

Perhaps to the extent that we have seen our own femininity redeemed, to that extent we can hope for more in other women. One evening when Dale and I went to sushi with Robin and Mark, Robin told me her secret. Her eyes darted around as if she were going to be caught. Then she whispered how even after seven years of marriage, she can't cook. Mark piped in and tried to explain how Robin feels pressured to cook well, especially in their small group that meets over meals. All the while, Robin kept saying how insecure she feels in the kitchen.

Dale and I kept throwing out unhelpful ideas like buying a rotisserie chicken at Costco and pretending you made it, and we laughed over it until Robin muttered under her breath, "I feel like I'm such a bad wife!" and stuffed another California roll in her mouth.

Later over coffee, Robin added that women in her small group really bug her when they put her in a box. "This last week they invited me to an all-day scrapbook party. They didn't even ask if I wanted to scrapbook or if I'm into that." She didn't try to hide her annoyance. "That's what bugged me, as if I only like scrapbooking. And to make it worse, the same day, all the guys are going biking to the beach."

I wondered out loud if she would have minded socializing with the other women had they been going rock climbing instead of scrapbooking. "Of course that would be different," Robin said. "Rock climbing is cool. It's fun!"

I thought about what she said and then drew two imaginary boxes in the greasy glass top of the coffee table. "It seems to me like you've taken all activities and put them into one of two boxes. One box, the male activities box, holds all the 'cool' things. They're the 'real world' things, the fun things." I indicated the left box. "Then you've got the 'uncool' things, which are the things women typically do: cook, clean, scrapbook, child care, wallpaper, garden, and so on. They're not cool, and they're definitely not fun."

At this point I started to smile, realizing I felt exactly the same as Robin. "So, we think we're better than those other women. We're above scrapbooking on Saturday. We're way more fun than that! And we think they're pretty pathetic for preferring scrapbooking to a bike ride to the beach."

Robin was smiling too. We saw ourselves. Because we both connected in our prejudice and because Robin is a gracious, open friend, she let me talk about how we think those women are pretty pathetic to spend all day in a room cutting pictures and putting pretty stickers on a page, when they could be cool and go to the beach. And how dare they lump us into their boring lives! By this point she and I were laughing loud enough to open up our souls to accept the problem. We didn't have to solve anything that night. It was enough that we saw it.

My conversation with Robin was the fruit of a meeting many months earlier with Sarah Sumner. I met Sarah first through her book *Men and Women in the Church*, and then at Mimi's Café. In her writings she seemed to understand what it meant to be a woman with unusual gifts. In seminary, one professor had told her, "Don't reveal the full colors of your plume ... guys will be intimidated." It was good to be understood by someone who had experienced prejudice in the church.

In one of her books, Sarah writes about a comment she made to a group of male pastors. In a backstage voice, she said, " 'You know how you feel you're superior to women because ... well ... you can just tell that you are?' And they all laughed. But what if I had said, 'You know how you feel superior to African Americans because ... well ... you can just tell that you are?' Do you think they would have laughed? I don't think so. It would have been a completely different matter. It would have been absolutely unacceptable to laugh. But women in the church, well that's another matter."

Sarah surprises me. She admits, with all her degrees and gifts and knowledge, to being prejudiced. Not against men, but against women. "I looked at myself and found the same prejudice for men there. In the big stuff, I preferred men. In matters of advice or seeking opinions, I valued males more then females. I sought men's approval. I took male leaders more seriously than women leaders. I valued my senior pastor's direction and expertise more than the Women's Ministries Coordinator."

I just stared at the page, feeling exposed. This woman was revealing our secrets.

"It's not that I wanted to be a man — I've never even for a moment wanted that. But I have wished in a wordless way deep inside my heart that I could somehow transcend my female self whenever I think that my womanhood has become a liability."

I saw where she was going, and I wasn't prepared to go there.

"Women prove they're above their female peers, they prove it in so many ways: when they compete, fight, succeed, keep up, debate, and discuss just like a guy." I saw a mirror looming up, reflecting me. I shifted in my seat. "We don't want to identify fully with the women we know and really love and value. Somehow we think it's an embarrassment."[4]

I'd had enough. I closed her book. I glanced around the coffee shop. On my right, an elderly couple was talking over their hot drinks. My eyes naturally focused on the man. I tried to imagine what he was talking about. His wife was looking at her fingernails. Subconsciously I had them pegged already. He was explaining something serious; she was thinking about her next manicure. He was rational; she was shallow. *No, no, no,* I caught myself. *Am I really prejudiced against women?*

Preferring Men: What Does It Reveal About Us?

A woman in a bikini walks down the beach, two men in tow. She believes that guys accept her for who she is, while girls are just jealous. The single woman at church returns from another disappointing women's retreat. She complains to her best guy friend: "They only care about their kids. I don't care about prom and soccer playoffs. Guys are just easier to talk to, because you care about the stuff that matters. I respect that a lot."

A mother confides in me: "Boys are easier to raise. They don't get in petty arguments. If my son is mad, he says so; but my daughter, heaven help us, she's little Miss Priss, holding grudges; you'd never believe her passive aggressive side. Sometimes I wish I had all boys."

One young wife tells me: "Men are more rational, they are natural leaders. Women are more emotional. I would be lost without my husband. I feel so sorry for the women who can't get married. How hard life must be for them!"

My friend who raises two children while maintaining her career in criminal enforcement once told me that men have it made. They don't have all these stupid obligations that women put on each other. When her junior-high son got into trouble this year, it was the women who suggested she quit to be home more. She's broken off most friendships with her female coworkers.

The pastor's wife tells my aunt: "I like you, you're more masculine, you say things as they are." The undercurrent is clear: women do not say things as they are, and if my aunt acted more like a woman, she would not be so likeable.

What do we subtly think and believe about other women? Do you value men's opinions more than women's? If you visit your church and learn that the pastor is out, but the Women's Ministries Leader would be happy to help you, will you listen and value her advice as much as the pastor's? If you find a female wearing an orange apron at Home Depot, will you trust her instructions on installing your sink? Or will you find a man?

Our prejudice isn't based on reality, because there are plenty of women who have proven how capable they are. Our prejudice is based on our flawed perceptions of femininity. We are still deceived about women—we believe that femininity is inferior, that womanliness is less than manliness, that women are not image bearers of God.

Hope in Women

After grad school, I audited a class on the theology of gender where I met Tiffany and Crystal—new companions on this path toward healthy femininity. We planned a lunch get-together. For the first fifteen minutes, Tiffany and Crystal complained of the common weaknesses of women. Tiffany finally asked, "Why do women still have all these problems? What holds them back?"

There were the general, appropriate answers like a history of misogyny, the ways men have abused women, the ways Satan has attacked them, the media, the airbrush artists, the dieting advertisements, and the church. But Tiffany had just finished writing a paper on those things. She knew all that. Wondering what she was really getting at, I asked her, "How do you feel about successful women who shine and use their power well and vibrantly?"

Crystal's honesty amazed me: "I don't like those types of women." Tiffany and Crystal looked glum and squirmed under the reality that we are part of the woman problem, that we prefer guys to girls, that we don't like the women who succeed and dazzle, that we distance ourselves from our own femininity.

Tiffany finally pierced the silence: "I know I'm part of the problem. I hate hanging out with girls. I mean, besides my closest friends," she gestured to Crystal. Both nodded and explained how girls backstab, ignore, demand, whine, and gossip.

It reminded me of my aunt (the same one who is called "masculine") who told me a bit of advice after I had a difficult run-in with an all-women's speaking venue: "After four decades of running a business in the corporate world, I can tell you that women will stab you in the back. Then, when you turn around, they'll kick you in the belly."

If I were to interview all Christian women, it would seem that the worst critics of femininity are not the men, but the women. According to most women, our vices far outstrip the men's. We are not women-haters. We are just, like Tiffany and Crystal, Bible-believing females who don't think women are quite as excellent as men. Why should we? We know how bad it can get. We are hungry for reasons to value our femininity, to remember the image of God that we were given in Eden.

Tiffany and Crystal were held back by their own beliefs about themselves. It's as if we all give silent assent to the belief that women are not as much full-blooded image bearers as men. Women just seem too petty, weak, and cursed. It's almost like we're wandering, homeless, wishing there was a way to rest in our womanhood. But we're too busy putting one foot ahead of the other, Emerald City in our sights, to stop and wonder what makes women valuable.

I thought about these women and their desire to understand femininity. I thought of our professor, Dr. Ron Pierce, who shared how he came out of limiting Christian women to freeing women to serve equally alongside men in the church. Dr. Pierce had begun to free me to understand how God values women. Then I had a small epiphany: "There is hope, though." Tiffany and Crystal looked up expectantly.

"You asked a woman to talk about these things. You chose me, not Dr. Pierce."

From there we began talking about the things we loved about the women we knew well, the women who had stuck with us through long stretches of change. We spoke of how we wound well, but how we can love well too. We talked of the sisterhood in Christ, the way interdependent and emotionally intelligent women have more ways to hurt, but also more ways to heal. Women can cultivate more customizations for their love. We, who have been forgiven much, can also love much.

We will find more reasons to trust the souls of women as we find reasons to see women redeemed by our God. If we look at Christ and bring our prejudices and doubts about femininity to him, we will see that he doesn't think woman can be summed up by "frailty."

Soul Care

1. What do you think of women who are single or childless? Do you value them, their wisdom, and advice more or less than those with children and grandchildren?
2. If you are interdependent, how have you abused this ability?
3. With whom are you unhealthily enmeshed?
4. Describe women you disrespect. How are you like them?
5. If you are sensitively aware, how have you wounded another with this ability?
6. What bothers you most about women?
7. What women do you admire? Why?

far as the curse is found

Christianity ... endowed the human female with a soul.

Simone De Beauvoir

god wasn't patronizing Eve when he let her in on Eden, offering her a seat as coheir with Adam. He wasn't breaking the entrance rules to let her join the party. "This is it, woman, my ground-breaking plan, and you and man will do it together—take care of this place." God called their role as caretakers "dominion."

If I had one phrase to describe that time, I'd call it the Fitted Age. Adam and Eve knew themselves, and they knew what they had to do. Those two, patriarch and matriarch, fit together and fit in Eden. And even better, Eve knew how well fit she was, not just for Adam, but fitted for her purposes, and for God's purposes. Eve knew that her body and soul matched in seamless perfection. Like a lake that stretches out to hold the magnificent sky without emptying itself of its own life and inhabitants, Eve was full of natural, unique thoughts, beliefs, emotions, desires, and choices. She was the only fully fitted feminine woman, and she was a picture of God to the world. There were no ripples distorting the image of God on her soul. And she knew it, self-possessed of her fitness without self-preoccupation. Out of Eve's self-possession, she could work with Adam and love him as his equal. She could provide for him without him feeling inadequate. She could take dominion and suggest and assert herself without anyone telling her to "let go and let God."

If Eve was beautiful, it was a beauty that bubbled from her inner soul to her body. Eve wasn't like so many women we know who are beautiful, poised, and good at socializing, but have about as much depth as a pie tin. Eve never did a double-take into her looking glass before bounding off to meet Adam. Her body reflected her soul, and her soul was not inadequate. I can barely imagine it. She must have been somewhat like the green lady we meet in C. S. Lewis's *Perelandra*, who is the Eve of her world, newly created and unblemished by sin. In *Perelandra*, the green lady is tempted as Eve was, but her response is different. Lewis's narrator deftly describes this green lady's self-possession and innocence. His words help me imagine Eve:

> Opposites met and were fused in a fashion for which we have no images. Neither our sacred nor our profane art could make her portrait. Beautiful, naked, shameless, young — she was obviously a goddess ... the alert, inner silence of those eyes overawed him; yet at any moment, she might laugh like a child, run like Artemis, or dance like a Mænad.[1]

Think about a time someone looked at you with depth and admiration. Maybe a guy noticed that you were different from the other girls in your class. Maybe he stopped dead in his tracks and looked at you, really looked at you. Remember the feeling of his eyes meeting your own, tightening your throat and stomach with excitement and pleasure over being seen and appreciated. And maybe for a moment, you enjoyed it without becoming self-conscious.

Eve lived there, in conscious delight of her fittedness. There was no disconnect between who man and God saw her to be and who she was. She fit the place. She fit her body. She fit her husband. She fit her God.

Ripples on the Lake

The day Eve started thinking twice about her fittedness was the day the first lie remolded her soul. It was the day she wondered if she really was enough. Maybe she needed a bit more. Maybe the tree was good for food, for wisdom. Maybe she could hold more of God if she ate some. Maybe she could better help Adam if she just took a little nibble.

Her soul rippled, the rings of her decision ricocheting through every capacity. And her eyes were opened; she didn't just believe a lie about her inadequacy, she really became inadequate. Sin moved from thought, to belief, to action, to reality. Eve became the thing she most feared.

Nowadays we blame her for every problem between the genders. It is because of Eve that we want to dominate. It is because of Eve that women are weak, frail things. Eve brought hierarchy in human relationships and made men the God-appointed, often reluctant dominators. Our new job, we are told, is not to take dominion, but to submit.

Lifting Parts of the Curse

In two areas of the curse, we've made some technological progress—through common grace—to minimize the pain. In agricultural labor and the labor of childbirth, we work to lighten God's curse. We don't think tractors and epidurals are wrong—we encourage all of these improvements. We want healthier and longer lives, which is why we hire medical practitioners, dentists, personal trainers, and pharmacists. It's why we get braces, shoes with arch support, lotion with vitamin E, and flu shots. We advocate medicine as if we were restoring something God originally intended, as if our medical advancements were participating in God's redemption of the world. We admire and promote reverses in the fall in the name of better health, better food, better lives. And we believe the kingdom of God is made manifest in these advances, that he is pleased with our ideas, and that he is blessing us through them.[2]

So why shouldn't we also seek to reverse that part of the curse that divides men from women? Why shouldn't we seek to undo the worst aspects of hierarchical gender essentialism? Why shouldn't we work alongside Jesus to restore men and women to harmonious partnership with one another? Is it because it's completely impossible, or is it because we don't realize that Christ wants to help?

Advent for Women

Around 3 BC, a man entered our world. His goal was not just to die, though that was on his to-do list. He didn't just drop down for the crucifixion. He came as a fetus, clinging to the womb of a young girl, waiting nine months before entering, wearing nothing at all. There was no spotlight or entrance music, no cameras, and certainly no central heating. My litter of puppies got better treatment.

He came to illustrate the immaterial, invisible, magnanimous soul of God. A child put it like this: "Jesus was the best picture God ever took." From flannel graphs to Bible study, we know he did amazing things. Just how much and how far did he redeem us?

If we were to sing the mighty hymn of "Joy to the World" from start to finish, we might realize this man cared about more than eternal life after death. As Isaac Watts knew and penned in 1719, there was more meaning in his death than release from eternal damnation.

No more let sins and sorrows grow,
Nor thorns infest the ground;
He comes to make His blessings flow
Far as the curse is found, far as the curse is found,
far as, far as, the curse is found.

How far do you think Christ's blood flows? Why is it that we fully accept Christ's sacrifice for our spiritual life, for our eternal lives; we even accept his common grace in agriculture and medicine, but we bar him from being our *Ezer* here and now in the gender war, in our frustration and frailty, and in our cursed femininity? Christ can redeem our true natures. But will we permit him to redeem us that far? Could Jesus lift women out of the female bits of the curse? Would it be all right? Can we ask him to lighten our load?

Forever Cursed?

When God cursed female desires in Eden, he changed an essential part of our souls. God told Eve that her desires would be permanently warped, her soul's capacity was debilitated.

"Your desire will be for your husband, and he will rule over you." The next time the word "desire" pops up is to describe sin's desire for Cain. "Sin desires you, it's crouching at the door, but you must master it."[3] We know how strong this desire was; it propelled Cain to slaughter his brother.[4] Many, many times I have heard that women's desires are now as demanding and warped as Cain's. Women desire to be in charge and dominate men, but God says we will be frustrated—perpetually frustrated. This is our curse. Submission, the lesson goes, is God's solution to woman's desire to rule, to keep women from demanding domination. God helps woman manage the repercussions of the curse by giving us the command to submit. This will keep women from barreling over the men.

Under this teaching, the curse still weighs heavily on us. Men might embrace tractors and women may accept epidurals, both can believe in the Lord Jesus Christ and inherit eternal life, but many continue to believe that women cannot receive relief from the curse about male rule and authority. Women have this peculiar, eternal curse to bear, a permanent mark much like Cain's, something they can never fully escape. So when a woman in Bible study is crying and frustrated with her husband, she might be told to lovingly, honestly submit. And when she returns the next week, feeling unable to correct her behavior, we all sympathize. We respond by saying, "It's the curse," and shake our heads over the sorry state of things. "It's just the curse."

That's it? That's the redemption? Jesus can give me eternal life, but he can't help me in my female soul, my identity here and now? We say we want Christ to come in and make us new, all the way to the center of our souls, but we really don't let him change this weight on women. We just settle for the feeling that this is our lot in life, hoping for better, but expecting a never-ending struggle with our identity and place as women. As a friend once wrote me, "Sometimes I feel that the gender struggle is going to be like a lifelong wrestling match where I get breaks between rounds, but it's never quite over. There are so many fighters in the ring all fighting each other for me — God, Scripture, the church, social theories, human rights activists, my gut."

And the fight within and without makes us doubt if our desires are even redeemable. We claim certain sins as part of the woman's makeup: we will forever be too easily deceived, hungry for a man, clamoring for attention, for beauty, for control. But what we're really saying is that these desires are too much for Christ to handle. We'd prefer to work it out of our souls with some extra scrubbing of blame, shame, and to-do lists. This is like the wizard's lie to Dorothy: "Before I will help you, you must prove yourself worthy." Is that what we're doing with our elbow grease, proving our worthiness by working out our domination with some willful submission? We keep walking our way along the yellow brick road, following the promise that if we just submit this time, we'll finally stop wanting control. It's the only cure we've been allowed.

The kind of submission that women work on perfecting is actually just covering up our soul's problems. It's like putting a Band-Aid on a dirty wound. It hides a problem that needs a good washing. Too often, submission means giving up or shutting down or hushing when our husband "feels more strongly" about something than we do. Deep down we're not submitting. I know it because I've heard us say things like, "I let him think he wears the pants" or "The husband is the head, but the woman is the neck" or "I'd rather submit to men, because I know how to work them; I can't work the women" or "Get him to think the idea is really his, then he'll do it."[5] It's faux submission, sanctioned by churches and husbands perhaps, but miles away from what Christ wants.

What must Christ think of this? It's like we're trying to scrub off our soul's problems with the wrong cleaner. We tell him — the God who knows precisely what he meant when he judged Eve — that this is our particular curse, that submission is to spend our lives scrubbing at it. This is our lot. To work against a desire for a lifelong domination pattern over men, muttering "thank-you-so-very-much, Eve" under our breaths and scrubbing away.

We keep hobbling on. We've squished ourselves into the wrong shoes, thinking silence means submission, that a gentle, quiet spirit means gentle, quiet vocal cords. We know our souls are aching, like our feet do after a long night in high heels. We are acting submissive without being humble or loving; we are expecting this makeshift bandage to carry us through life. Then, as some teach, when we finally die and are fully remade, we will accept subordination in heaven without a fight.[6]

Why are we convinced God specifically wants to curse women more than men? It might make us wonder at the unfairness of God to give women something to bear forever when men can be redeemed with Jesus and a tractor.

Redeeming Fallen Femininity

When Jesus appears on earth in Bethlehem, it is as if the playwright has walked onto the stage. Jesus is even more familiar with the opening lines in Genesis — and the first curses — than we. He lives, dies, and rises to meet the last lines of the curse and, in C. S. Lewis's words, "Death itself starts working backwards."[7]

Jesus redeems our bodies, promising his friend Martha that if she believes in him, she will never die.[8] Much like in Narnia when the statues in the White Witch's courtyard slowly come alive, we are being made alive by the God-Man. Eternal life starts now. Our bodies will catch up later.

Jesus redeems our souls. We find the evidence in his dealings with one woman in Bethany whose desires point us in a different direction. She is a woman who may or may not have been married. Her marital status, her fashion sense, her finances, her cooking skills, her serving skills, her sewing skills, her hospitality, her figure, and her children, if she had any, have little import next to her one overarching desire. Of her desires, this we know: "Mary has chosen the good part, which shall not be taken away from her."[9] Jesus said that there is one desire that never needs stifling, squishing, or stuffing. In Mary of Bethany, Jesus gave us a chance to see what he could do for women.

Mary, sitting with the disciples, near enough to touch the God-Man's feet, was able to fill her soul's desires. There is only one thing needed and she grasped it. Her sister did not get it: Martha wanted to serve a good meal, but Jesus told her, in effect, "No, Martha, change your desires and grow into life abundant." Mary and Martha did not need beauty or a boyfriend, not sons or daughters. They needed a new desire. The head of the church, who heads us all, married or unmarried, virgin young and old, worn-out mothers and independent aunts, the ravished, the jilted, the wealthy, and the depressed, provides a fresh wash on our desires. As he says in Revelation, he has come to make all things new.

We might know that Christ can make all things new, but perhaps we haven't trusted him for it. Or perhaps we haven't thought about how Christ can redeem us from the full weight of the judgment. We might be like Dorothy sitting in the witch's dungeon, wearing the ruby slippers, but still crying, "I'm trying to get home, Aunt Em, I'm so frightened, I'm so alone." If we feel homeless or alone, perhaps we haven't fully seen the power we have been given and the Man on the journey with us.

The curse, the captivity, is over. Our desire to dominate or rule a man can be saved and remade. As Christ redeems our bodies from death, so he also wants to redeem our souls. He told us we can have the right desires right now, the ones he can fulfill, the ones that are never taken away. Mary chose that. We can choose that too. We can desire him. And in walking with him, we will never know corsets or false and flimsy ideals of femininity. Jesus never denigrated or belittled the difference in women. He never told them to hush, or to stop asking for so much, or to keep away from his teaching. Jesus never hinted in a sermon or miracle or act that there was anything irredeemable about woman's nature. As Dorothy L. Sayers put it:

> Perhaps it is no wonder that women were first at the Cradle and last at the Cross. They had never known a man like this Man ... A prophet and teacher who never ... flattered or coaxed or patronized; who never made jokes about them ... who took their questions and arguments seriously; who never mapped out their sphere for them, never urged them to be feminine or jeered at them for being female.[10]

In his words to Mary, God showed how he can give us a new set of desires to enjoy and explore and grow into. These new desires will spill into new beliefs, feelings, and choices and renew our spirit.

Redemption after Eve

So does it work? Could Christ redeem me now from a fretful, overwhelming desire for my husband, from the fears I have that one day he might be taken away? For the first few years of our marriage, Dale traveled with an itinerant ministry. In our pre–Welsh Corgi state, I waited alone at home with two Siamese cats for company. At night in a big empty bed, I would wonder and fear the things that might happen to him. Leaving him at the airport was the hardest. I would fight back a spring of tears as I gave him the hurried hug and drove off from him, always afraid that this may be the last time. Would I ever see him again, or was that the last good-bye?

Recently, a married friend confided an almost identical fear. What if our husbands die? What would we do? How do we keep this fear from crippling us and leaking dark oil into our soul's capacities? How could we go on in this life? Doesn't this prove that our desire for our husbands is still overwhelming?

She reminded me of the words of C. S. Lewis in *The Four Loves*. If Dale died, I would long for him to love and to be loved by him again. The color would drain from my life. But even Dale, glorious husband that he is, is a rivulet of the original fount of love.[11] The best and deepest love we find on earth is a portrait of the original. Dale is an image bearer tutoring me to long for his original. Depending on the character of my love for Dale, I will more fully recognize the Maker of my love. When I die, it will not be this earthly beloved that I seek, though I expect to be standing shoulder to shoulder with Dale marveling in our God. We were made for God. As Augustine says: "We are restless until we find our rest in him." It is only in mirroring God that any earthly lover could excite and attract us. It is only in being like the glory, kindness, and love of God that my husband could have drawn me to himself.[12]

When we see the face of God, we shall know that we have always known it. He has been a party to, has made, sustained, and moved within, all our earthly experiences of innocent love. In heaven we will finally turn from those God made loveable to the source, to Love himself.[13]

This is what Mary chose, and this is what we can choose. Our desire to love and be loved by God can never be taken away from us. We can, in fact, love God *through* loving our husbands. In loving Dale well, I am loving God well.

Jesus asks for intelligent, earnest, long-obedience-in-the-same-direction commitment from women as much as he does from men.

It was a new desire for women, not another thing Mary added to her list of duties that day. It was not something she had to work on — no, it was something Jesus gave to her. He created a new desire in her, to hunger and thirst after the kingdom of God. Mary chose Christ, and he began to lift the curse. He creates new desires in us much like a friend elicits a desire to be with them, much the way my husband creates the hunger for me to accompany him, even on long, dark Jeep trails with nothing but his company to keep me steady. I want to be with him.

Mary wanted God. And when I pay attention, I see that *I* want God, more than I want to be with friends, more than I want to be in control, more even than I want to be reunited with my husband after long trips away. My desires are being made anew, they are being fulfilled. My desire is being fulfilled, and as Solomon says, it is "a tree of life."[14]

I am becoming more free. Not free to live out my dominations or check off my lists or squeeze into a corset. But free to be more like the triune God, the way he has redeemed me to be: fully female, fully human.

Jesus in Female Form

I asked Jesus to transform the abused, embarrassing, dishonest understanding I had of submission. I asked Jesus to show me how he would submit. And he redeemed the idea for me, not by telling me submission no longer applied to me, not by removing the task, but by showing me how God is made great when I bend my knee. He taught me how submission is actually much more, not less than, I had been trained to believe. He showed me that submission begins with knowing myself so that I might more fully and maturely give myself to others. He showed me how the verses on submission are often preceded by verses on image bearing. Take Colossians 3:10, eight verses before a submission passage: "Put on the new self who is being renewed to a true knowledge in the image of its Creator." In this renewal there is no distinction.[15] The old gender wars and ethnic barriers are gone. I yield because I am like God when I yield.

God has shown me that submission is much more than letting my husband make all final, big, spiritual decisions (a strange distinction since all decisions really are spiritual). Submission doesn't mean giving up; it means that all decisions are a group effort, without wheedling, cold silences, or halfhearted surrenders. Submission is about working to be vulnerable with my husband.

God showed me that I get to submit, not as an exercise of stuffing my desire to dominate, but because my life is so much bigger than dominating anyone. Submission lets me be God to others. Carrying a pack for two miles, is how Jesus put it. Submitting to others for God's sake is just one picture of how God is here in his body on earth. I get to determine what God would look like if he were to step into my shoes in this moment. How would God live as a married woman in Los Angeles who loves to garden, has three Welsh Corgis, and writes and speaks on femininity? How would God live if he were a single woman in a big city? Does he wear that, walk like that, believe that? Does God stay silent in churches, letting his abilities go overlooked? Does he request opportunities to speak? If so, how does he do it?

If God were an athletic woman, what would he dress like? Where and how would he work out and hang out with the guys at the gym? If God were a beautiful woman, how would he use his beauty? If God were a mother, how would he look to the growth of his children while being intentional about growing his own soul? If God were a wife, what view would he have of submissive love? Can you imagine God being submissive? What would that look like if he were married to your husband, in your house, in your kitchen, in your job? How much more gracious, or more firm and uncompromising would he be? How much more gentle and less nagging would he be? What would God do in a female body?

Offering God Our Shards

Women are reflective glasses of God. We hold his image right this minute. Though we begin life as cracked pictures, it is God who holds all our pieces. He holds mine and he holds yours.

God watched and grieved as the young boy mocked my hair. He watched as my soul was seared by a broken engagement. And God sealed those pieces back together. There are scars, but I reflect him in that too. We serve a God with scarred hands.

God groans as we fixate on the romantic love that we think we are cursed to demand. He wants to redeem our soul's desires with something that will never be taken away. God shudders when I remake submission into the hardhearted, rigid, clay-soiled coil of control and manipulation, but he works my clay until I am capable of cultivating a culture of life again. And being Grace himself, he mends the splinters we send into others' mirrors too.

When I approach Dale in humble love, I am Jesus to him. When I submit without canceling my soul's gifts and capacities, I am being Jesus to the world. When I love without demanding that I alone must meet that need, I am being Jesus to my family. When I absorb the evil, like blood in a sponge, I am being Jesus to my friends.

Jesus wants to redeem the feminine resemblances in each of us. Our female bodies can be transformed from seductive, weak, distracting fashion models into vulnerable vessels of grace. Our souls can grow from dependence to interdependence, from rigid defensiveness to sensitive awareness, from domination to emotional intelligence, from nagging manipulation to cultivation. We bring ourselves to him, and each time, the triune God moves his hands over our brokenness, re-glues, realigns, and seals us in himself, so that we as women hold his image, again.

The idea that Jesus came to rework the shades of Eden into glorious masterpieces is not new. But it has been cloaked or forgotten for a long time.[16] When Paul said there is neither black nor white, upper or lower class, male or female, he distinguishes himself as the first person in the history of our planet's literature to argue that all human beings are equal.[17] Not until the 1980s did evangelicals formally embrace the spiritual equality between men and women.[18]

This is what Jesus came to do — to die and rise so that there might be both equality and difference in us, all the way to our souls' femininity and masculinity. His death can still make a difference in the everyday, hum-drum war between the sexes.

A Snail's Pace

There is a little running shop in Brea, California, called *A Snail's Pace*. I've always liked the name, even before I shopped there, because it seems to value steadiness more than speed. I'd heard from friends that the clerks will invite you to sit down, gather an enormous stack of running shoes, and begin fitting you for the best pair. You put a pair on, hike up your pant cuffs to your knees, and then run back and forth. The clerk watches your foot strike to determine if you roll in or roll out. I'd heard of how helpful they were, and though I've been running for years, it took me more than a decade to try them out.

I walked into *A Snail's Pace* and explained to the sales clerk that I was slightly pigeon-toed. I explained all my foot problems, the way my feet were small but wide in the front and narrow on the heel, how new shoes rarely fit. He got me to roll my cuffs up, watched me run in the shoes I had on, asked me my shoe size, told me I could roll my pant legs down again, and then disappeared. He was on a quest for the perfect running shoe. I sat skeptically until he returned a few minutes later with five boxes, all of which, he assured me, would correct my stride, and all of them one size larger than what I had told him. I protested over the big shoes.

"Trust me," he said, "you will need more room. When you run, your feet swell and your toes need the space. If you get shoes that 'fit' like you're used to, your toes will get bruised. Your toenails might fall off."

I quieted down, even though I was certain he was wrong. But since he was supposed to be the expert, I put the shoes on, stood up, and rocked back and forth sinking my heels and toes into the soft, loamy cushions. The shoes were roomier than I expected—there was indeed room to grow and swell. But I smugly explained to him that my heels slipped out. Unimpressed, he took my shoe and with a clever lacing trick, tightened the opening. Roped securely in, I was instructed to jog around a bit. After several practice laps around the store, I was sold.

Later that day, I put on my new shoes and took a walk. Everything felt different. I imagined the earth tremble and lift me at each stride. It was a Douglas Spaulding moment, from when he buys his tennis shoes in *Dandelion Wine*. After the walk, I noticed my feet had precious few indentation marks from laces or seams. These were shoes that really fit.

Why hadn't I been fitted for running shoes sooner? I had bought lots of shoes in the last four years, most of them beautiful, heeled things, short-term dandies, great for about thirty minutes. But then they'd pinch and rub, and at best, strain my stride. But beauty is pain, right? Sometimes you just have to ignore it, because a woman must look confident in her heels, at all costs, even at the cost of the skin on her feet. I've already done damage to my feet, my left foot has a crushed nerve between two of the bones, I've permanently smashed nails, reshaped toes, endured backaches and fatigued calves all for that certain look. Some women are getting wiser and refuse such shoes. My sister sported flip-flops to her prom—smart cookie.

Ruby Slippers Fitted for Us

I'm beginning to pick out those rare women who refuse to push their souls into places that cramp and constrict them—not because they're rebellious or prideful, but because they know they cannot walk with Jesus like that. Some of them tell me they've learned from calluses and scars on their souls, from years of forcing their souls into ill-fitting roles. It is time to throw out the wrong meanings of submission and femininity. It is time to act in trust that, for Christ, there is a mind to be built, emotions to be owned, and a will to be directed. He can redeem our desires.

What would happen if women everywhere accepted their femininity, their ruby slippers? What if we took our cue from Christ and walked into roles that fit us, supported us, and still left room to swell? The swelling might mean we choose to be married or have children; we might be widowed or divorced. Our boyfriend might leave, our sister might move to the other end of the house, our mom might avoid us. Our goals might change, we might lose our jobs. The swelling might mean old age, cancer, or stretch marks. But with redeemed souls, this swelling won't ruin us, because you and I have a flexible understanding of femininity, enough to grow our souls without losing our womanhood.

We have the space to develop our minds without losing our natural femininity in the process. We can discover how feminine we are before adolescence and into old age. We can suffer breast or ovarian cancer without feeling our femininity is at stake. We have been given the clearance to grow our emotions and cultivate our desires without our God dismissing us as unstable. We have that fresh, loamy space to experience gracious freedom in our souls.

I think Jesus wanted that kind of freedom for us, to give us shoes that don't limit where we can go, or force contorted arches or mincing steps on our journey. He holds out these comfortable ruby slippers fitted to our soul's femininity. He explains that they're red because he paid dearly for them to fit us. Will you let him wash your bruised and bloody feet? Will you accept them?

Come to me weary and heavy laden one, and I will give you rest.

Take my yoke upon you and learn from me, for I am gentle and humble at heart.

And you shall find rest for your souls.[19]

epilogue

the journey of ruby slippers

I began writing *Ruby Slippers* intending to describe all women with just three words, believing this method could capture the woman's soul. My ideas, however, were another corset, tying women to one narrow definition. I had fairly good motivations. I wanted to vindicate misunderstood Paul who must have had a reason for warning women against usurping authority over men. I planned to encourage women to embrace their role, to accept their proclivity toward being easily deceived, and to own their soul's differences. I expected to find some ontological difference in women's souls, a difference proving why we must not expect authority or leadership. For the first year, I dug up confirming articles in psychology and theology. The data is there if you want it. Scientific, psychological, and theological history is replete with studies "proving" women's inadequacies.

But writing is a curious discipline; it calls us to the carpet when we are dishonest. As the sun rose and set over my keyboard, I grew less content with my thesis. I felt niggling feelings that more than a few women did not fit my neat list of words — women as close as my grandmothers, my friends, my literary agent, my mother-in-law, and Mary sitting at Christ's feet.

Had I stuck with my original idea, *Ruby Slippers* would have been an atrocious little book. But in 2005, one year after I started this project, my ideas began changing. Psychologists, theologians, and authors challenged me to re-think my thesis.

In the spring of 2005, *Captivating* was released and began buzzing around churches. I eagerly and anxiously read it, wondering if the book I was working on had already been published. As I pored over it, I realized that though the Eldredges' writing was appealing, their book suffered from something I wanted to avoid — the add-woman-and-stir approach. It comes out of using a model of maleness as the starting point. I grew more convinced that I needed to delve deeper into myself and into women. I wanted to be certain to dignify woman as made in God's image in ways that went beyond romance and beauty, to include those women who didn't fit the *Captivating* model.

Out of all these encounters, I refashioned *Ruby Slippers*. I've tried to maintain depth without compromising accessibility. I've attempted to dignify women's variety and creativity and intelligence. I've aimed to integrate psychology, theology, philosophy, history, women's studies, and my own walk with Christ into a primer on the woman's soul. You will judge if I have been helpful.

More books need to be written on the feminine soul. Work needs to be done to uncover additional family resemblances in femininity. More exercises need to be developed for caring for our soul's strengths and growing out of our weaknesses. We need Bible studies that refuse to stereotype and that integrate soul care into theology.

In the meantime, I hope *Ruby Slippers* has given you fresh direction toward a freeing, full-blooded femininity.

Jonalyn Grace Fincher, MA
December 30, 2006
Whittier, CA

notes

Introduction: Femininity beyond Fairy Tales

1. Gender (the socio-cultural invention) is usually distinguished from sex (the biological given). Here I am using them interchangeably to mean both body and soul differences within men and women.
2. Although there is an inequality among headship positions (men dominate as headmasters, principals, and vice principals) and a disproportionate distribution of men in the hard sciences, female teachers experience more equality in pay and time off, regardless of their gender.
3. Mary Kassian, *The Feminist Mistake* (Wheaton: Crossway, 2005), 20.
4. Adolf Hitler at a women's rally in Nuremberg, 1936, taken from the official party proceedings, "Die Tagung der deutschen Frauenschaft," *Der Parteitag der Ehre vom 8. bis 14. September 1936. Offizieller Bericht über den Verlauf des Reichsparteitages mit sämtlichen Kongreßreden* (Munich: Zentralverlag der NSDAP, 1936), 161–69 as quoted at http://www.calvin.edu/academic/cas/gpa/pt36frau.htm.
5. Renée Altson, *Stumbling Toward Faith* (Grand Rapids: Zondervan, 2004), 112.
6. Elaine Storkey, *What's Right with Feminism* (Grand Rapids: Eerdmans, 1985), 119.
7. Henri J. M. Nouwen, *The Return of the Prodigal Son* (New York: Doubleday, 1992), 37.
8. Rob Bell, *Velvet Elvis* (Grand Rapids: Zondervan, 2005), 150–51.
9. Serene Jones, *Feminist Theory and Christian Theology: Cartographies of Grace* (Minneapolis: Fortress Press, 2000), 8.
10. In philosophical terms, I am speaking of femininity as an essential property to every woman.
11. 1 Corinthians 14:34; Proverbs 31:26.
12. 1 Timothy 2:12; Judges 4:4.
13. Proverbs 31:27; Esther 4:14–16; 2 Kings 22:14–23:3.

Chapter 1: Materialism for Women

1. C. S. Lewis, "The Weight of Glory" in *The Weight of Glory and Other Addresses* (New York: Collier Books, 1975), 16.

2. Wendell Berry, *Hannah Coulter* (Washington, D.C.: Shoemaker and Hoard, 2004), 10.

3. Jane Austen, *Pride and Prejudice* (London: Octopus Books Limited, 1983), 29.

4. Elizabeth von Arnim, *The Enchanted April* (London: Virago Press, 1922), 87.

5. Matthew 6:22–23.

6. Matthew 7:2.

7. www.collegeclub.com.

8. Dave Matthews, "Crash Into Me," *Crash* (New York: RCA, 1996).

9. This concept is adapted from Lauren F. Winner's *Real Sex: The Naked Truth about Chastity* (Grand Rapids: Brazos, 2005), 70–77.

10. Matthew 23:26–28; Luke 11:43–44.

11. George Orwell, "Notes on the Way" in *The Collected Essays, Journalism and Letters* (London: Secker & Warburg, 1968).

12. Jesus said, "You blind Pharisee, first clean the inside of the cup and of the dish, so that the outside of it may become clean also" (Matthew 23:26).

Chapter 2: Uncorking the Soul

1. Luke 8:15.

2. Matthew 22:37.

3. John 4:24, Jesus's words to the Samaritan woman. It is tender of the Redeemer Man to speak such theology to a woman. Men in his time wouldn't have entrusted such ideas to women.

4. Mormons believe God has a body. Neo-pagans (Wiccans, pantheists) believe the earth is God's body. Muslims, Christians, Jews, and Deists believe God does not have a body.

5. Genesis 2:7. See text note.

6. Genesis 1:20–23, 26–28 MSG. I'm glad this text was written originally in Hebrew because they differentiate between singular and plural pronouns. In Hebrew, the language is quite clear that both men and women were involved in this creation mandate, "Man and Woman, subdue and rule the earth together."

7. "All things have been created through Him and for Him. He is before all things, and in Him all things hold together" (Colossians 1:16–17).

8. Judges 10:16 (see note); Genesis 1:2. Usually, though not always, Scripture uses "spirit" to talk about a powerful immaterial force while "soul" means an immaterial essence.

9. *Nephesh* can also mean various body parts, like the mouth (Isaiah 5:14) or neck (Psalm 105:18). But when *nephesh* refers to God, it can't mean anything physical, since God isn't made out of physical parts.

10. Matthew 22:37.

11. If you are interested in a longer explanation of the different ways *nephesh* and *ruach* are used, see J. P. Moreland and Scott B. Rae, *Body and Soul: Human Nature and the Crisis in Ethics* (Downers Grove, Ill: InterVarsity, 2000), 23–33.

12. Alvin Plantinga, "Advice to Christan Philosophers," *Faith and Philosophy* 1 (July 1984): 264–65.

13. 1 John 4:19.

14. Genesis 6:6.

15. Isaiah 55:8. This often quoted passage is frequently misused to mean that we can't understand how God works, that he is so beyond us. But in context it means that God's mercies often betray our own stingy portions of grace. See the verse prior to this, Isaiah 55:7. God sets the standard, as his judgments are always right, so his mercy is always deep, deeper than our thoughts of mercy, especially for others.

16. Psalm 139:17.

17. Job 1:8.

18. Hosea 10:10.

19. 2 Chronicles 7:12.

20. Isaiah 42:1.

21. God even experienced sensation when the second person of the Trinity took on flesh and stepped into the material world.

22. This is why studying the Bible more than other books is a good idea. It is a sneak peak into reality, better than our own conjectures. It is also the best picture on the soul of God.

23. You don't need a body to experience pleasure. A good story can give us mental pleasure, a good choice can give us satisfaction that isn't physical, a memory can bring us emotional pleasure.

24. Philippians 2:6–7.

25. Philosophers call these "faculties." "A faculty is a compartment of the soul that contains a natural family of related capacities" (Moreland and Rae, *Body and Soul*, 204).

26. For more on the potency of the soul, see *Body and Soul* by Moreland and Rae.

27. Richard Swinburne, *The Evolution of the Soul* (Oxford: Clarendon Press, 1997); Dallas Willard, *The Renovation of the Heart: Putting on the Character of Christ* (Colorado Springs: NavPress, 2002).

28. Scripture often compares our belief process to seeing light or darkness. The light opens our eyes to the truth and the darkness dims our eyes to the reality of God's world (2 Corinthians 4:3–6).

29. A sensation can also include things you think you sense, like hallucinations. A person's perceptions are their reality, which is why we need a community to learn truth. I can ask my friend, "Is that a person or a tree?" That's why "a matter must be established by the testimony of two or three witnesses" (Deuteronomy 19:15 TNIV; John 8:17). Moses and Jesus thought it was a good idea.

30. Willard, *Renovation of the Heart*, 30.

31. 1 Corinthians 9:24–27; 10:13; Philippians 3:12–14; and Hebrews 12:1.

32. J. P. Moreland, class lecture, Spiritual Foundations of Ministry Lab, spring 2002.

33. Willard, *Renovation of the Heart*, 38.

34. "For it is God who is at work in you, both to will and to work for His good pleasure" (Philippians 2:13).

35. Charlotte Brontë, *Jane Eyre* (Mineola, NY: Dover, 2003).

36. The spirit is what philosophers call a second order faculty. Our spirit looks in on all our capacities, such as our thoughts, beliefs, desires, feelings, and will. The spirit is like our soul's evaluator, allowing us to step back and examine where we are, where we are going, and what we're going to do about it. Socrates was talking about this introspective knowledge—or the spirit, as I'm using it here—when he said, "Know thyself."

37. Soul: "At night my soul longs for You, indeed, my spirit within me seeks You diligently" (Isaiah 26:9). Evil spirit: "Test the spirits" (1 John 4:1); "By this we know the spirit of truth and the spirit of error" (1 John 4:6). Immaterial substance: "A spirit does not have flesh and bones as you see that I have" (Luke 24:39). God: "The Spirit of God was moving over the surface of the waters" (Genesis 1:2). Heart: "Therefore my spirit is overwhelmed within me; My heart is appalled within me" (Psalm 143:4). Emotions: "How is it that your spirit is so sullen that you are not eating food?" (1 Kings 21:5). Will: "For the LORD your God hardened his spirit and made his heart obstinate" (Deuteronomy 2:30); "Renew a steadfast spirit within me" (Psalm 51:10).

38. Proverbs 20:27 TNIV.

39. 1 Corinthians 2:10–11 NLT.

40. Harriet Lerner, *The Dance of Anger* (New York: HarperCollins, 1985), 112.

41. If women are not souls, then any amount of abuse can be justified against them. It should always prick our ears if we hear someone robbed of her soul-hood. For instance, from history, Aristotle believed women's souls were rationally defective. Today the Nandi in Kenya believe a woman must share her husband's soul since she doesn't have one. Some Muslims obey the words of Mohammed who said, "Men are superior to women on account of the qualities with which God hath gifted the one above the other" (*Qur'an*, sura IV, verse 38). In India, the gender selective abortions account for upwards of 10 million missing females. This devaluing of women continues today in China and Vietnam.

42. Placide Clappeau wrote "O Holy Night" in 1847.

43. Remember that Scripture uses "heart," "soul," and "spirit" interchangeably to mean will, emotions, mind, or immaterial part.

Chapter 3: The Same Planet

1. Exodus 18:4.
2. Deuteronomy 33:7.
3. Deuteronomy 33:29.
4. Psalm 20:2.
5. Psalm 70: 5.
6. Psalm 115:11.
7. Psalm 121:1–2.
8. Psalm 146:5.
9. Thomas Hopko, "On the Male Character of the Christian Priesthood," in *Women and the Priesthood* (New York: St. Vladimir's Seminary Press, 1983), 106.
10. For every study we do of Genesis 2 with the unique beginning of woman, we must re-read Genesis 1 where God puts his image in both of us. See Genesis 1:27–28, write it on your mirror, set it as your screen saver, abide in that truth.
11. Charlotte Perkins Gilman (1860–1935), from Juliette Clark and Helen Exley, eds., *Women's Thoughts: Quotations Selected by Helen Exley* (New York: Exley Giftbooks, 1996), 28.
12. "Reasons for Employing Women as Telegraph Clerks" suggested in 1871 by Frank Ives Scudamore as quoted in Fiona Macdonald, *Women in Nineteenth Century Europe* (New York: Peter Bedrick Books), 39.
13. Storkey, *What's Right with Feminism*, 23.
14. "The 50 Women to Watch," *Wall Street Journal*, November 20, 2006.
15. Gustave Le Bon as quoted in Carol Tavris, *The Mismeasure of Women* (New York: Touchstone, 1993).

16. Storkey, *What's Right with Feminism*, 23.
17. See David Murrow's *Why Men Hate Going to Church*, Lean J. Podles's *The Church Impotent: The Feminization of Christianity*, or Holly Pivec's "The Feminization of the Church" in *Biola Connections* at http://www.biola.edu/admin/connections/articles/06spring/feminization.cfm.

     Perhaps a better criticism would be that the church is pandering to the fallen forms of femininity, or that the church is faltering. Instead of insulting women, it would be more helpful to keep the gender accusations out of it altogether. Women have a hard enough time loving their femininity without this.
18. Psychologist Carol Gilligan says the biblical story is part of woman's problem and the beginning of sex discrimination: "Adam and Eve—a story which shows, among other things, that if you make a woman out of a man, you are bound to get into trouble. In the life cycle, as in the Garden of Eden, the woman has been the deviant." *In a Different Voice* (Cambridge, Mass.: Harvard University Press, 1982), 6.
19. "Female humanity is just as human as male humanity, even though the two are distinctive." Sarah Sumner, *Men and Women in the Church* (Downer's Grove, Ill: InterVarsity, 2003), 67.
20. Galatians 3:28.
21. Robert Nadeau, *S/He Brain* (Westport, Conn.: Praeger, 1996), 60.
22. Janet Shibley Hyde's tool is meta-analysis, a process that pulls all relevant studies (in this case, on gender difference), adds them together, and averages the cumulative research to determine psychology's overall, general findings.
23. Janet Shibley Hyde, "The Gender Similarities Hypothesis," *American Psychologist* (September 2005): 581–92.
24. Including reading comprehension, vocabulary, spelling, language, verbal reasoning, abstract reasoning, talkativeness, smiling while aware and not aware of being noticed, facial expression processing, negotiating outcomes, leadership, gregariousness, and self-disclosure to friends and strangers.
25. Including perceptual speed, space relations, mental rotation, spatial visualization, throw velocity, throw distance, sprinting, computer self-efficacy, mechanical reasoning, and progressive matrices.
26. Including numerical ability, mathematical self-confidence, computation, mathematical concepts, problem solving, and mathematical anxiety.
27. Including interruptions in conversations, intrusive interruptions, assertive speech, physical and psychological verbal aggression, aggression

in low emotional arousal contexts, aggression in real world settings, indirect aggression, competitiveness, self-esteem, depression, motor behaviors, and moral reasoning.

28. Hyde, "The Gender Similarities Hypothesis," 587. See also Carol Tavris, *The Mismeasure of Women*, 41–42 for a similar example in mathematics.

29. Movie preferences are, by far, one of the worst ways to prove gender norms. For one thing, individuals vary so much over movie tastes, and our desires for a romantic or violent flick are often the result of unhealthy idealism or voyeurism more than evidence of natural, God-ordained differences.

30. The love is not agape here. It is the Greek *phileo* (*philandros*), the kind that requires time and cultivation to build (see Titus 2:4–5).

31. 1 Corinthians 7:8–9. Observe who pursues the man in Song of Solomon 3:1–2 and who wants to bed whom. Among several excellent, honest points in her speaking and writing, Shannon Ethridge promotes some common cultural lies, one that sexual intimacy and sight stimulation is a man's thing and emotional intimacy and auditory stimulation is a woman's thing. See *Every Woman's Battle* (WaterBrook, 2003), 13.

32. For instance, the left-brain, right-brain lore that passes as science tends to make rigid, non-overlapping hemispheres, when actually, both sides of the brain participate in most activities. They are not completely clear opposites, nor are they dominantly gender specific. The corpus callosum, a bridge connecting both hemispheres, doesn't necessarily indicate that women's hemispheres are more integrated than a man's. In Hyde's look at studies, documenting over 1.4 million people, she found that there were no gender differences in verbal skills. For a history of the contradictory, oscillating findings behind gender differences, see pp. 45–56 of *The Mismeasure of Women*.

Chapter 4: Leaving Eden

1. You can find more at http://buriedtreasurebooks.com/PrairieMuffin-Manifesto.php.

2. Altson, *Stumbling Toward Faith*, 176.

3. Mark Ellis preached on this idea in his sermon, spring 2006.

4. Thanks to Dr. Walt Russell's insight of tweaked compasses in his spring class, Hermeneutics, 2002.

5. Rebecca Groothuis, "Equal in Being, Unequal in Role" in *Discovering Biblical Equality* (Downers Grove, Ill.: InterVarsity, 2004), 301.

6. Living as real humans, not blaming our humanity (as in, "Well, I'm only human") is the resolution behind Soulation, the nonprofit that

Dale and I began in 2005. Soulation exists in order to help people "walk into being appropriately human," to claim their humanity as their birthright. See www.soulation.org.

7. Sibylle von Streng, trans. Sr. Allison Braus, "Woman's Threefold Vocation According to Edith Stein" in *Women in Christ* (Grand Rapids: Eerdmans, 2003), 111.

8. "Not that I have already obtained it or have already become perfect" (Philippians 3:12).

9. Romans 8:29.

10. 2 Corinthians 3:18.

11. "It was not Adam who was deceived" (1 Timothy 2:14).

12. John Milton, *Paradise Lost* ed. Roy Flannagan (Boston: Houghton Mifflin, 1998), Book 9, 1.1121–31.

13. Milton, *Paradise Lost*, Book 9, 1.1010–55.

14. Natalie Imbruglia, "Torn," *Left in the Middle* (New York: RCA, 1997).

15. See the king of Egypt holding Abraham, not Sarah, responsible in Genesis 12:18–19.

16. Genesis 3:16.

17. Genesis 3:20.

18. Ischomachus is lecturing his wife in Xenophon's *The Economist*.

19. Cicero, "For Murena," in *Orationes*, 12.

20. Plato, *The Laws*, 7.

21. Demosthenes, "Against Neaera," in *The Orations*, 9.

22. According to Freud, she lacked that "essential" organ.

23. Little wonder Dan Brown's religion looks "better" and enticing; he's dismissed the gnostic's chauvinistic doctrines. But that's what boutique religion is, cozy but inconsistent. The closing statement of the Gospel of Thomas has Simon Peter saying, "Let Mary leave us, for women are not worthy of life." Jesus says to him, "I myself shall lead her in order to make her male, so that she too may become a living spirit resembling you males. For every woman who will make herself male will enter the kingdom of heaven." Translated by Thomas O. Lambdin, *The Gospel of Thomas*, 114.

24. Augustine, "Literal Commentary on Genesis," as quoted in Elizabeth Ann Clark and Thomas Halton, *Women in the Early Church* (Collegeville, Minn.: Liturgical Press, 1984), 28–29.

25. For Augustine, "The woman together with her own husband is the image of God, so that the whole substance may be one image; but when she is referred to separately in her quality of helpmate, which regards

the woman herself alone, then she is not the image of God; but as regards the man alone, he is the image of God as fully and completely as when the woman too is joined with him." Augustine, "On the Holy Trinity," Book 12, Chapter 7 as quoted in Julia O'Faolain and Lauro Martines, eds., *Not in God's Image: Women in History from the Greeks to the Victorians* (New York: Harper, 1973), 129.

26. 1 Peter 3:4.

27. Mary Wollstonecraft, *A Vindication of the Rights of Woman* (Mineola, NY: Dover, 1996).

28. I'm alluding to the radical, secular feminist movement. There have been several women's liberation movements. Feminism itself should be distinguished with an adjective to separate secular, liberal feminism, Marxist feminism, radical feminism, and Christian feminism. Christians would do well to distinguish the differences when they speak against or for feminism as this would prevent further misunderstanding. Not all feminists are angry females out to crush men or prove their superiority.

29. I would make a distinction between "secular feminism," which fails to notice God's hand in making humanity, and "Christian feminism," meaning a concern for women's welfare and advocacy for her equal human status as an image bearer of God.

30. There is an important, but often ignored question about the intersexed (a person born with ambiguous genitals), or more derogatorily called hermaphrodite, person. Intersexed are often permanently damaged because doctors and parents force a sex on them at infancy, even though most will gravitate toward one gender by adolescence. So how should we respond to those intersexed persons whose genitals remain perpetually ambiguous? I would say Christians ought to be the first to validate them as full human souls with all their capacities intact, though with marks of the fallen world on their bodies. Perhaps this is what Christ meant when he said in Matthew, "For there are eunuchs who were born that way from their mother's womb" (19:12).

31. Matthew 22:37; Mark 12:30; John 11:24–26.

32. 2 Samuel 14:25; see also verses 26–27.

33. Beauty is also not the essence of God any more than truth, love, strength, and grace.

34. Mary Stewart Van Leeuwen, *Gender and Grace: Love, Work, and Parenting in a Changing World* (Downers Grove, Ill: InterVarsity, 1990). Perhaps because she has seen the abuse of the difference, she believes men and women are the same in terms of soul. Though I disagree with

her on this point, I can see why she would fear or even disbelieve in a soul difference.

35. Ibid., 69.
36. Eugene Peterson, *Run with Horses: The Quest for Life at Its Best* (Downers Grove, Ill.: InterVarsity, 1983), 13.
37. Romans 8:22.

Chapter 5: A Natural Woman

1. Eugene Peterson, *Run with Horses*, 13.
2. Karl Barth, *Church Dogmatics*, 201–2.
3. Pope John Paul II, *Evangelium Vitae* (1995), par. 99.
4. Beth Moore, *Believing God* (Nashville: Broadman and Holman, 2004), 42–43.
5. There is, of course, a list of natural masculine family resemblances.
6. A sex change doesn't affect this either. Men with female-constructed body parts have not altered their souls.
7. This is perhaps the most egalitarian statement in Scripture: "The wife does not have authority over her own body, but the husband does; and likewise also the husband does not have authority over his own body, but the wife does. Stop depriving one another" (1 Corinthians 7:4–5). We have the opportunity to give our bodies to one another.
8. Owens deftly illustrates and struggles with the identity she feels with her body. This short story covers her encounter with a lump in her breast, her mother's Parkinson's, and her daughter's horror at old ladies' bodies. In the end, she refuses to surrender her questions to the TV commercials or her HMO. It is this kind of honest body attention that women need to practice together. "The Message in the Body," *Image: Art, Faith, Mystery* 48 (Winter 2005): 90.
9. Leslie Brody, *Gender, Emotion and the Family* (Cambridge, Mass.: Harvard University Press, 1999), 11.
10. Hanna-Barbara Gerl-Falkovitz, "Gender Difference: Critical Questions Concerning Gender Studies" in Michele Schumacher, ed. *Women in Christ* (Grand Rapids: Eerdmans, 2003), 4.
11. The Greek word for "weak" is *asthenēs* which literally means "strengthens." See 1 Peter 3:7 ESV.
12. 1 Timothy 2:9–15.
13. "And He has said to me, 'My grace is sufficient for you, for power is perfected in weakness.' Most gladly, therefore, I will rather boast about my weaknesses, so that the power of Christ may dwell in me" (2 Corinthians 12:9).

14. *Asthenēs* again in 1 Corinthians 1:25.

15. *Asthenēs* in both instances in 2 Corinthians 13:4.

16. Dr. Sumner showed me how God and women share this same attribute of vulnerability. See her excellent explanation in her chapter "What's a 'Weaker Vessel'?" in *Men and Women in the Church* (Downers Grove, Ill: InterVarsity, 2003), 131–35.

17. Sumner's question at the end of chapter 11, "How do you suppose," she asks, "women's bodies affect women's way of thinking and women's behavior?" makes me realize much more work still needs to be done on soul care for women (*Men and Women in the Church*, 138).

18. Bono said this at the National Prayer Breakfast in 2006.

19. I'd make my case with Genesis 1:26–28; 3:16.

20. Some could argue that woman's vulnerability makes it necessary for a man to direct us in all significant aspects: home, church, and community. It may be fitting, godly, and most Christlike in many cases to yield, but I beg to differ that our vulnerability makes us "natural followers." Furthermore, men are also weak, or vulnerable. Women are just more *physically* vulnerable.

21. Janelle Hallman, "The Glory of Gender" in *Love Won Out* (Pasadena, Calif.: Focus on the Family, 2001).

22. I'm not saying woman was physically weaker. It is possible woman was just as strong as man before the judgment.

23. I don't want to assert that women are relational because they are made out of living flesh. I'm merely suggesting that woman's physical makeup is a possible symbolic picture of the life of Eve, the mother of all life. It is not a clear biblical truth (no biblical writer ever says, "Woman is made out of a living being, she is therefore more interdependent"); rather, this idea is merely a symbolic extrapolation of the Genesis text, not a description of the way all women are.

24. Hallman, "The Glory of Gender."

25. Mike Mason, *The Mystery of Marriage* (Sisters, Ore.: Multnomah, 1985), 149.

26. 1 Corinthians 12:22–23.

27. I am not speaking of emotional stripteases before men we are trying to reel in, nor physically exposing ourselves in unsafe places. This soul vulnerability is something that I think begins with honesty about who we are and what we fear.

28. In John 13:3–4, Jesus says that it is because he knows who he is, that is, from the Father and that he returns to the Father, that he can lower himself and serve like this.

29. If you read John 13:1–5, you can see the thought process Jesus used to motivate himself to get down on his knees in front of his disciples, even his betrayer.

30. See Ephesians 1:3.

31. With the rest of the family resemblances, I've relied on psychological studies more than brain or neural evidence. The way our souls use our bodies is often more spiritually significant than our neurology or brain functioning.

32. Carol Gilligan's psychological work, *In a Different Voice*, sparked a new awareness of women's differences. She suggested that all women have these differences. Some of her discoveries, like interdependence, ethic of care, and connected knowing are more common in women, but I would not say all. Gilligan has drawn severe and consistent criticism, especially from her peers, for claiming that all women are interdependent and connected knowers, while men are not (Cambridge, Mass.: Harvard University Press, 1982), 13.

33. It is not only women who are connected knowers. To connect in order to know is human. Women may just have a head start on this.

34. Connected knowing starts with personal interaction, but it doesn't end there. The mode of knowing is personal, the object of knowing doesn't have to be. You can be a connected knower in the way you understand a painting ("What was Van Gogh feeling when he painted *Starry Night?*"), a book ("I heard my voice in it"), a garden (Job said, "Listen to the earth and it will teach thee"), a passage in Scripture ("It spoke to me"). No wonder the ancients peopled the earth with spirits, gods, and goddesses. They felt like they were engaging personalities in the world, not just inanimate things.

35. Mary Belenky et al., *Women's Ways of Knowing* (New York: Basic Books, 1986), 113. For a different perspective, one that finds cultural factors as greater predictors of connected vs. separate knowing than gender, see Michelle K. Ryan, Barbara David, and Katherine J. Reynolds, "Who cares? The effect of gender and context on the self and moral reasoning" in *Psychology of Women Quarterly*, vol. 28, issue 3 (September 2004): 246–66.

36. Acting like a separate knower may be as intimidating for some women as it is for some men to launch into connected knowing. We must understand the difficulty of moving into a different mode of knowing for every person. It cuts both ways: some women naturally prefer separate knowing and some men prefer connected knowing. Separate and connected knowing are not gender specific, though they may be gender

related. I have run across more men who are separate knowers and more women who are connected knowers, but I won't shove all men into one box, or all women into the other. (For more, see Belenky et al., *Women's Ways of Knowing*, chapter 6.)

37. Freda Mary Oben, trans. *Essays on Women*, 2nd rev. ed., vol. 2, *The Collected Works of Edith Stein* (Washington, D.C.: ICS Publications, 1996).

38. In this study, participants were asked to frown or smile for ten seconds. Their heart rate and skin temperatures showed larger changes than when they re-created anger or happiness merely in their imaginations. Ekman, Levenson, and Fiesen, 1983 from Leslie Brody, *Gender, Emotion and the Family* (Cambridge, Mass.: Harvard University Press, 1999), 17–18.

39. Martin, Harlow, and Strack, 1992 from Leslie Brody, *Gender, Emotion and the Family* (Cambridge, Mass.: Harvard University Press, 1999), 18.

40. G. K. Chesterton, *Orthodoxy* (Wheaton: Harold Shaw Publishers, 1994), 49.

41. "The Real Princess," *Fifty Famous Fairy Tales* (Racine, Wis.: Golden Press Western Publishing Company, Inc., 1965), 242–43.

42. As quoted in *USA Today*, Elizabeth Weise, "Men, Women: Maybe We are Different," August 22, 2006.

43. One test for emotional sensitivity is called the Profile of Non-Verbal Sensitivity (PONS) where individuals are asked to identify the emotion displayed by different actors. In PONS, women outperformed men from countries as different as New Guinea, Israel, Australia, and North America. Simon Baron-Cohen, *The Essential Difference: The Truth about the Male and Female Brain* (New York: Basic Books, 2003), 32.

44. In technical terms, 33–84 percent more men than women are physically aggressive, 9–55 percent of men are more verbally aggressive, and while 5 percent of men use indirect aggression, up to 74 percent of women are more indirectly aggressive. Again, notice how nonuniversal these percentages are. There is such wide overlap.

45. Angela Thirkell, *Wild Strawberries* (New York: Carroll and Graf, 1937), 105.

46. I'm certain one could argue that I am sensitive because of my mother's nurturing, but then I notice my sister who is not particularly sensitively aware, but who is a feminine, gracious woman. There is more behind sensitivity than upbringing.

47. 1 Timothy 5:10.

48. 1 Timothy 5:14.

49. Keeping house was also much more empowering in the first century; it wasn't denigrated as unpaid or woman's work. The matron of the Roman house was called *domina*, from which we get words like "dominate" and "dominion." This *domina* was her husband's associate in religious affairs. She was his companion in the workplace. Cato, a Roman historian writing a few centuries after Christ, knew the power of a *domina* when he wrote, "Everywhere men rule over women, and we who govern all men are ourselves governed by our women." See Simone de Beauvoir, *The Second Sex* (New York: Vintage Books, 1989), 93. Cato knew that women often have a natural gift in governing the home and the lives of others. And God knew that too, which is why he inspired Paul to promote women's work at home in the first place. Women are not, in my mind, relegated to the home any more than a man is to the marketplace. Both men and women need labor beyond the home to grow their souls. The home is not, after all, any more sacred than the marketplace (see Colossians 1:10; 3:23).

50. I've heard women's sensitivity distinguished as "womanly intuition," but that's not quite grand enough. Intuition is limited since it only describes our awareness of other people's nonverbal cues. Sensitive awareness can also be a help to knowing ourselves. It is a trait that our spirits use to introspect and more fully know ourselves.

51. Dr. Sara E. Snodgrass looked at sensitivity as found in real-life interaction, comparing men's and women's beliefs about their working partner's feelings and comparing them to what their partner actually claimed to feel. She wanted to get at the answers to these types of questions: How does she feel about what I said? Is he feeling self-confident in this task? See her article "Further Effects of Role Versus Gender on Interpersonal Sensitivity" in *The Journal of Personality and Social Psychology*, vol. 62 (January 1992).

52. A moderate amount of teen girls and women exceeded teen boys and men in things like smiling while being observed (295 different summaries). A large amount of women of all ages differed from men over casual sex (10 summaries). And in adolescents and adults, a large amount of females over males were more sensitive or "tender minded" (10 summaries). Hyde, "The Gender Similarities Hypothesis."

53. One study found that baby girls looked longer at faces, especially eyes, while baby boys looked longer at inanimate objects, like mobiles. This was true of babies only one day old. See the study in Simon Baron-Cohen's *The Essential Difference*, 55–56.

54. Emotionally intelligent people are often skilled in emotion-laden language, things like metaphor, simile, poetry, song, fable, dream, and myth. Daniel Goleman, *Emotional Intelligence: Why It Can Matter More Than IQ* (New York: Bantam, 1995), 54.

55. Dunn, Bretherton, Munn, 1987 from Leslie Brody, *Gender, Emotion and the Family* (Cambridge, Mass.: Harvard University Press, 1999), 36.

56. Shimanoff, 1983 from Leslie Brody, *Gender, Emotion and the Family*, 36.

57. Goleman is a philosophical materialist (he only believes in the material world) so he fails to credit emotions as a capacity of the soul. He thinks emotions are a key part in human survival (*Emotional Intelligence*, 43–44). I see Goleman as a pagan prophet, discovering truth in spite of his inability or unwillingness to know its Author.

58. Goleman, *Emotional Intelligence*, 34.

59. Ibid., 49.

60. Women report a higher degree of sensitivity to lower volumes of sound. Women tend to notice variations of saltiness, bitterness, sweetness, and sourness in foods. Women tend to be able to pick up smells quicker than men, and women are more sensitive to alcohol. See Tara Parker-Pope's "The Case Against Ladies Night: Drinking Has Hidden Health Risks for Women," *Wall Street Journal*, December 26, 2006.

61. "You have taken account of my wanderings; Put my tears in Your bottle; Are they not in Your book?... This I know, that God is for me" (Psalm 56:8–9).

62. Willard, *Renovation of the Heart*, 30.

63. Ibid., 34.

64. Raising children, however, is not something unique to the soul of a woman either. God makes parenting the dominion of both sexes; we are supposed to work together on it. He doesn't claim women are more nurturing than men, nor that mothering (as we define it: picking up the toys, wiping dirty bottoms, cutting fingernails, preparing food) is the exclusive dominion of mothers. In Isaiah 1:2, God indicates that he is a parent. "Sons I have reared and brought up." If parenting is not beneath our Father in heaven, then why is it often beneath husbands on earth? Parenting (in my naïve and unpracticed opinion), no matter how messy, sticky, snotty, or tedious, is the dominion of both sexes.

65. Not until after the curse does Man name Woman Eve, the "mother of all the living" (Genesis 3:20).

66. Maybe it's because women can be mothers, though I don't think that's the exclusive reason that many women are constantly cultivating life. Motherhood is one way to describe it, but I think it's an insensitive title, especially for childless females. Edith Stein said women seek and embrace whatever is "living, personal, and whole. To cherish, guard, protect, nourish, and advance growth is her natural desire." As quoted by Laura Garcia, "Edith Stein—Convert, Nun, Martyr," www.catholiceducation.org/articles/religion/re0001.html. Stein would say this was true of all women, though I'd nuance it to say it's true of many.

67. *American Heritage Dictionary of the English Language*, 3rd ed. Electronic Version (New York: Inso Corporation, 1996).

68. Freda Mary Oben, trans. *Essays on Women*, 132.

69. This doesn't mean such a man could not exist.

70. Edith Stein, "Die ontische Struktur der Person," as quoted in Michele Schumacher, ed. *Women in Christ* (Grand Rapids: Eerdmans, 2003), 114.

71. Another helpful metaphor for describing woman's soul is the earth, as in woman is like the ground: organic, life-making, multidimensional, interdependent, sensitive, aware, cultivated, and cultivating, etc. The metaphor intrigues me because of the Greek's Ceres, the neo-pagan's Earth Goddess, the Egyptian's Isis, and the true story of Eden's Eve, but especially because I'm a gardener.

Chapter 6: Finding the Feminine in the Sacred

1. To hear the talk that evening, see "She's Got Soul" at www.soulation.org/library.html. Look under "Theology."

2. French philosopher as quoted in Nancy Reeves. *Woman Beyond the Stereotypes* (Chicago: Aldine, 1971), 101.

3. I am indebted to Sarah Sumner for many of these observations. See *Men and Women in the Church*, 121.

4. John 1:2.

5. John 1:14.

6. Matthew 28:18.

7. Madeleine L'Engle, *Walking on Water: Reflections on Faith and Art* (Wheaton: Harold Shaw, 1980).

8. A provocative thought experiment I batted around with Christian philosopher Dr. William Lane Craig is to think of what the world would have to be like if the Logos incarnated as a woman, the Daughter of God. There are several reasons to think he wouldn't, such as the system of sin resting on the males (the first and second Adam), the Jewish

culture prohibiting a woman acting as high priest, Palestine's culture during the first century forbidding women from learning, and then there are the prophesies foretelling a male Messiah. But could the Logos have done so, provided the Godhead rearranged aforesaid hurdles, if the Logos chose to? This idea clearly needs more thought, research, and dialogue.

9. Colossians 1:16.

10. Psalm 131:2.

11. Deuteronomy 32:3–4, 6.

12. Deuteronomy 32:18.

13. Isaiah 42:14.

14. Isaiah 49:15.

15. Isaiah 66:9–13.

16. Though I think it's worth our time to try to understand those who do, especially if they call themselves followers of Jesus.

17. There are good reasons not to call God "Mother": God did not reveal himself as mother to the ancient Israelites, lest they begin to worship the many fertility goddesses their neighbors worshiped. And God does not reveal himself as mother to us today. If God were mother, then God becomes rather too close to creation, birthing us in a way so literal that we would lose some of God's transcendence; we would lose the crucially important distinction between the Creator and his creatures.

18. Debbie Blue, *Sensual Orthodoxy* (Saint Paul, Minn.: Cathedral Hill Press, 2004), 36.

19. "The Spirit also helps our weakness; for we do not know how to pray as we should, but the Spirit Himself intercedes for us with groanings too deep for words" (Romans 8:26).

20. He packs our bag "with every spiritual blessing in the heavenly places" (Ephesians 1:3).

21. Jesus said it best, "I have come that [you] might have life" (John 10:10).

22. Renée Altson, *Stumbling Toward Faith*, gives a chillingly honest picture of what she endured as her father raped her while reciting the Lord's Prayer. In her book, part of her healing is found in this prayer: "O ruach elohim/ feminine/ spirit of God, who/ pushes back darkness/ chaos/ leaving space/ for birth/ for creation/ O ruach/ feminine/ spirit of God who/ breathes out hope/ life/ making space/ for safety/ for untangling knots/ for creating/ new paths/ O ruach/ feminine/ spirit of God/ I beg you/ please/ hold me." She shares how the gender-neutral Bible renewed verses that she had memorized as only for the men; "brothers" was

now "brothers and sisters." She was able to believe that she was really included. See page 150.

23. "And a woman who had had a hemorrhage for twelve years, and had endured much at the hands of many physicians … hearing about Jesus, she came up in the crowd behind him and touched His cloak … Immediately Jesus, perceiving in Himself that the power proceeding from Him had gone forth, turned around in the crowd and said, 'Who touched My garments?'" (Mark 5:25–30).

24. One direction will always need editing, and sometimes complete renovation, as in the case of women whose fathers abused them.

25. Job 33:4.

26. Genesis 28:3. For more, see http://www.bible.org/netbible/isa13_notes. htm.

27. Genesis 49:25.

28. F. Brown, S. R. Driver, and C. A. Briggs, *A Hebrew and English Lexicon of the Old Testament* (Oxford: Clarendon Press, 1907).

29. John 14:2.

30. Luke 13:34.

31. Matthew 11:28–30, my paraphrase.

32. One helpful phrase for understanding the Trinity is: Three "who's" (Father, Son, Spirit), one "what" (God).

33. Some would say, "Well then, add a fourth and a fifth." But while a second and a third add different qualities of agape love, I don't see how any more would. More persons would add quantity of love, but not a different quality. See the full argument developed by Richard Swinburne, *The Christian God* (Oxford: Clarendon Press: 1994).

34. Ephesians 3:5.

35. Luke 4:1, 18–21.

36. John 17:3; Luke 1:35; Philippians 2:7.

37. John 10:17.

38. Acts 2:24. See text note. "Agony" in Greek is *odin*, which means a pang, especially of childbirth.

39. John 14:16. James Strong, *The Exhaustive Concordance of the Bible* (Peabody, Mass.: Hendrickson Publishers, 1988), 79.

40. I used to believe my desire to help and fix and change things was just another place I needed to "let go and let God." This is a helpful suggestion when we need to stop managing others' emotions, but it isn't particularly helpful when we need to do some honest soul care and manage our own emotions, thoughts, beliefs, and desires.

41. Milton, *Paradise Lost*, Book 11, 1.165–169.

Chapter 7: Frailty, Thy Name Is Woman

1. Men's vices might well be understood as their strengths gone bad. For instance, a man who refuses to expose himself for those he loves might make up for his weakness by acting barbaric, chauvinistic, dominating, abusive, or overly aggressive. Just as women are afraid to be vulnerable, perhaps men are also afraid to be exposed.
2. "Your wife shall be like a fruitful vine within your house, Your children like olive plants around your table. Behold, for thus shall the man be blessed who fears the LORD" (Psalm 128:3).
3. Jinjur's female Army of Revolt in *The Marvelous Land of Oz*, 1904, sequel to *The Wonderful Wizard of Oz*, L. Frank Baum and John R. Neill (New York: HarperCollins, 1985).
4. Sumner, *Men and Women in the Church*, 70–79.

Chapter 8: Far As the Curse Is Found

1. C. S. Lewis, *Perelandra* (New York: Scribner, 2003), 64.
2. I am using "kingdom of God" as Dallas Willard means it in the *The Divine Conspiracy*. The kingdom of God is the effective range of God's will, where God's will is effectively implemented.
3. "If you do well, will not your countenance be lifted up? And if you do not do well, sin is crouching at the door; and its desire is for you, but you must master it" (Genesis 4:7).
4. Genesis 4:10.
5. In J. M. Barrie's play, one woman sports this false, smug submission: "Every man who is high up loves to think that he has done it all himself; and the wife smiles, and lets it go at that. It's our only joke. Every woman knows that." She may know it, but to hide it, or play the joke on our husbands, is hardly loving submission. From *What Every Woman Knows* (Mineola, NY: Dover, 1997), 34.
6. See John Piper and Wayne Grudem, eds., *Recovering Biblical Manhood and Womanhood: A Response to Evangelical Feminism* (Wheaton, Ill.: Crossway, 1991), 176.
7. C. S. Lewis, *The Lion, the Witch and the Wardrobe* (New York: HarperCollins, 2005).
8. Jesus chooses a woman, a capable housekeeper like Martha, to give this teaching to: "I am the resurrection and the life; he who believes in Me will live even if he dies, and everyone who lives and believes in Me will never die. Do you believe this?" (John 11:25–26). He honors her will and mind as a female image bearer of God.

9. Luke 10:42.
10. Dorothy L. Sayers, *Are Women Human?* (Grand Rapids: Eerdmans, 1971), 68–69.
11. C. S. Lewis, *The Four Loves* (San Diego: Harcourt, 1991), 137–39.
12. Ibid., 139.
13. Ibid.
14. Proverbs 13:12.
15. NASB with TNIV.
16. George Fox, with his wife, Margaret Fell Fox's guidance, rejuvenated Paul's teaching in the seventeenth century. The Friends or Quakers claimed it as one of their distinctives. "For Man and Woman were help meets in the Image of God, and in Righteousness and Holiness, in the Dominion before they fell; but after the Fall, in the Transgression, the Man was to rule over his Wife; but in the Restoration by Christ, into the Image of God, and his Righteousness ... they are help meets, Man and Woman, as they were before the Fall." George Fox, 1672, *A Collection of Many Select and Christian Epistles*. Fox's words come from Margaret Fell Fox's 1666 pamphlet, the first to argue for woman's spiritual equality to man. See her *Women's Speaking Justified, Proved and Allowed of by the Scriptures*, written during her four-year imprisonment.
17. As historian Timothy Cahill writes, "Most of us should be cheered that here, plunk in the middle of this old-hat stuff about what to wear, we have the only clarion affirmation of sexual equality in the whole of the Bible—and the first one ever to be made in any of the many literatures of our planet." See *The Desire of the Everlasting Hills* (New York: Anchor, 2001), 141.
18. The first to do so was the group Christians for Biblical Equality in 1987 with their statement "Men, Women and Biblical Equality." The second, right on its heels, was "The Danvers Statement" in 1988.
19. Matthew 11:28–30, paraphrase.

recommended resources

The first book listed in each section is most recommended.

Freedom in Femininity

~*Kiss Sleeping Beauty Good-bye: Breaking the Spell of Feminine Myths and Models*, Madonna Kolbenschlag

~*The Mismeasure of Women: Why Women Are Not the Better Sex, the Inferior Sex or the Opposite Sex*, Carol Tavris

~*Stumbling Toward Faith: My Longing to Heal from the Evil God Allowed*, Renée Altson

Soul Care for the Mind

~*Love Your God with All Your Mind*, J. P. Moreland

~*Renovation of the Heart*, Dallas Willard

Soul Care for Emotion, Desire, Will

~*The Dance of Anger: A Woman's Guide to Changing the Patterns of Intimate Relationships*, Harriet Lerner

~*In Quiet Light: Poems on Vermeer's Women*, Marilyn Chandler McEntyre

Soul Care for the Spirit

~*Changes That Heal: How to Understand Your Past to Ensure a Healthier Future*, Henry Cloud

Soul Care for the Female Body

~*Eve's Revenge: Women and a Spirituality of the Body*, Lilian Calles Barger

~*Real Sex: The Naked Truth about Chastity*, Lauren F. Winner

Philosophy for Women

-*Are Women Human?* Dorothy L. Sayers

-*The Second Sex*, Simone de Beauvoir

Theology for Women

-*Discovering Biblical Equality: Complementarity without Hierarchy*, eds. Ronald W. Pierce and Rebecca Merrill Groothuis

-*The IVP Women's Bible Commentary*, eds. Catherine Clark Kroeger and Mary J. Evans

-*Men and Women in the Church*, Sarah Sumner

-*Men and Women in Ministry: A Complementary Perspective*, eds. Robert L. Saucy and Judith K. TenElshof

-*When Life and Beliefs Collide: How Knowing God Makes a Difference*, Carolyn Custis James

History of Women

-*No Time for Silence: Evangelical Women in Ministry Around the Turn of the Century*, Janette Hassey

-*Not in God's Image: Women in History from the Greeks to the Victorians*, eds. Julia O'Faolain and Lauro Martines

-*A Return to Modesty: Discovering the Lost Virtue*, Wendy Shalit

-*What's Right with Feminism,* Elaine Storkey

Psychology

-*Gender and Grace: Love, Work and Parenting in a Changing World*, Mary Stewart VanLeeuwen

-*In a Different Voice: Psychological Theory and Women's Development*, Carol Gilligan

acknowledgments

In this adventure through Oz, I did not write alone. There were intelligent scarecrows, tender tin woodsmen, bold lions, enthusiastic munchkins, faithful Kansas citizens, wizards, good witches, and, of course, wicked witches too.

My Loyal Toto: Dale, who worked hard to understand femininity through all my alterations, who has pulled me away from perfectionism and self-blame, rushing me to our favorite sushi restaurant, who sought help when I was in the clutches of wicked witches, and has kept me from flying away with wizards in hot air balloons.

My Glinda: Agent 003 who welcomed me to Oz. Thanks for appearing at just the right times and showing me the path to Zondervan.

My Brilliant Scarecrows: Dr. Liz Hall, who gave psychological insight and Dr. Sarah Sumner, who gave theological honesty. These two women were sharp enough and concerned enough to challenge my harmful version of femininity.

My Tin Woodswomen: Angela, editor and kindred spirit who shows gentleness for all women on the yellow brick road; Becky, who divided my manuscript's wheat from chaff; and Abigail, sister and friend, who took time to axe out unhelpful ideas in my first five chapters and offer her steadying advice.

My Bold Lions: Dr. Ron Pierce and Dr. J. P. Moreland, men who were courageous enough to honor my mind as a woman, who refused to dominate or patronize my book aspirations.

My Munchkins: those willing, able readers who have given me the gift of their time, reading through my entire book before it went to press: Dale, Mandy in New Jersey, Lori in Ohio, Lisa in Alabama,

Paula in California, Katherine in Maryland, and Tiffany in Colorado. Thank you for helping me finish.

My Aunt Mae: my mother who regularly sent me books and newspaper clippings, who worked up beautiful graphics for the text, and who kept track of my soul as I changed. I'm glad we are remaking our friendship.

My Kansas dwellers: anchors to the real world who championed me through Oz. In Oregon: The Holmans for being the first to encourage my roughest of rough drafts. In New Jersey: The Orozcos for offering emotional and philosophical honesty. In New York: Faith McCormick for her willingness to help me with graphic design. In Virginia: Stephanie Kopalchick who offered the most powerful tool a mother of two can give—steady, sensitive prayer. In Canada: Susan Lawrence for maintaining that pipeline to God when I was too weary to pray. In Los Angeles: Mama Grace for her emotional zeal and intelligence, Jeff Lefever for volunteering to befriend and believe in the Finchers, Adam Stowell for telling me that this book would be writing me, Karen Pierpoint who helped me connect my writing to my life, and Grandma Taylor for introducing me to Dorothy in the first place.

soulation™

sturdy answers. better souls.

Soulation exists to navigate ideas, stir imaginations and help others become appropriately human.™

Soulation is the husband wife team of Dale and Jonalyn Fincher. With backgrounds in the performing arts, history, literature, theology and philosophy, they cast apologetics wider than evangelism and academic debate. Working both as a team and individually, they build whole, hearty souls: sound emotions, sturdy beliefs and strong wills. Their itinerary takes them around the nation to churches, public and private schools, conferences, camps and universities.

www.soulation.org